Praise For The Demise of Labor

"This extraordinary book should be required reading for all students, teachers, employers and employees in all industries and institutions of learning. Changes in labor laws, job markets, and today's workforce make this book a must read. Brian hits the nail on the head with his true-to-life account of what workers are looking for today, and his crusade to help employers and employees find success all while sifting through the political land mines of labor unions.

— *Dr. Mathew Friedman PHD, Doctor of Economics*

The DEMISE Of LABOR

The Brian Ahakuelo Story

Book design by:
Arbor Services, Inc.
www.arborservices.co/

Printed in the United States of America

The Demise of Labor: The Brian Ahakuelo Story
Brian Ahakuelo

1. Title 2. Author 3. Business Management

Library of Congress Control Number: 2017906527
ISBN 13: 978-0-692-88472-0

The DEMISE Of LABOR

The Brian Ahakuelo Story

BRIAN AHAKUELO

This book is dedicated to my beloved wife, my children and their spouses, and my grandchildren. You have helped me to see what is truly important in life.

Acknowledgements

I would like to thank my parents, the late Norman and Rowena Ahakuelo, for the faith and fortitude they instilled in me. Without them, I would not have had the strength to survive this journey.

Contents

Introduction

Mornings had always been my favorite time of day at the office. I liked to get in early, five a.m. or so, to gather my thoughts and prepare for the day before everyone else got there. But that Friday, May 6, 2016, only I and Marilyn, Local 1260's director of community services and my wife of thirty-five years, were in. It was the start of Mother's Day weekend, and I had emailed the rest of the staff that Wednesday and told them to take the day off.

I might have taken the day too, but for a meeting I had with Harold Dias, the International rep for District 9 of the International Brotherhood of Electrical Workers (IBEW). Promptly at eight, I went over to meet him at the door. Harold Dias walked in, dressed in his usual aloha shirt and khakis. Behind him stood Mike Grunwald, another International rep, and John O'Rourke, the VP of the district, both dressed in suits and ties. I was surprised to see them, especially O'Rourke, for he was based in San Francisco and normally let me know when he was in town.

I stood up to shake their hands. "Good to see you, Mike . . . John."

"Brian," O'Rourke replied cordially, but said nothing about his reason for being there.

Still, I thought nothing was amiss as we left the entrance of the office and headed for the conference room which, like the rest of the space, overlooked the Pacific. Staring out the window at the blue vastness, you could almost forget the bustle of downtown Honolulu sixteen floors below. The office itself was open and airy and cream-colored throughout, a far cry from the office I had been left with when I became business manager of Local 1260 in 2011. Later, when the shock wore off, I would begin to see the irony that against the beautiful backdrop I created, my thirty-five-year relationship with the IBEW would come to an abrupt end.

We took our seats at the conference room table, then without preamble, O'Rourke went into his bag, took out a piece of paper, and slid it toward me. I looked down, my eyes widening at the sight of the words "International Charge." When I looked further, I saw other words too, something about financial malpractice—malpractice I had allegedly committed.

I looked up at the three men across from me, no longer seeing my colleagues but a hit squad. Harold and Mike found other places to look, but John met my gaze head-on.

"Are you guys serious? John, what's this about?"

"Well, Brian, you know there are the complaints from 2011."

I knew them well. These complaints had been lodged when I was elected to my first term as business manager. The incumbent and his handful of followers, angry that I had unseated him, had made some allegations against me in the hopes that management would call for another election or, at the very least, that my reputation would be damaged before my tenure even began. Instead, the complaints were investigated and found to be "frivolous and without merit." Three years later, I ran against the same man again, this time with a successful record to stand on, and easily defeated him. As for his allegations, they were never mentioned again; in fact, I had not been approached by the leadership about any suspected wrongdoings.

"Have there been more recent complaints?"

John shook his head.

"So no charges whatsoever?"

Another shake of the head.

"So why are you doing this, John?"

I saw the slightest flicker, then a hint of a smug smile.

"Because I can, Brian."

For a split second, I thought about punching him in the face, anything to make that smile disappear.

"You and Marilyn have three minutes to grab what you can from the office."

Marilyn? How did they even know she was there? Before I could ask them, they were on their feet and heading toward Marilyn's office, with me in tow. When John gave her the news, her look of shock matched my own. After being married to me—and therefore the IBEW—for over three decades, she was well-versed in union politics, but this was beyond the pale.

Without a word I went back to my office and grabbed the few things I could carry; the rest of my personal items would be packed up by whomever came in to comb through the offices. Then, like two perps being carted off to jail, Marilyn and I were marched to the elevator bank. Before stepping into the car I met Harold's eye. Sixteen years of shared history passed between us and faded just as quickly.

"Brian, I knew nothing about this," he said, and I don't know what angered me more, the fact that he was lying or the fact that after all this time he didn't think I could tell.

Marilyn and I rode silently down to street level. Outside, the world looked the same as it always did—sun shining, traffic flowing smoothly down the pristine, palm-tree lined street—but after what had just happened, it seemed almost perverse. Although Marilyn and I didn't say it, we both knew we were leaving the building on 700 Bishop for the last time.

That didn't meant the union was through with us; far from it. By that evening, my "crimes" had been plastered all over the local news media. Auditors from the national offices in Washington, DC, were going through the office computers, gathering "evidence." As I listened, shell-shocked, to the list of charges leveled against me, it was like hearing about a stranger. Who was this "embattled union boss"?" Surely it wasn't me, the guy who had grown up in the union hall and who had spent, literally, all of my adult life serving its members. I thought about all the times I'd heard about someone on the news—a politician, a union boss, the CEO of a company—and assumed what the media reported was true. Now, as I listened to some news anchor coldly describe me as a criminal, or at least unethical, I realized how naïve I had been. In the past few hours, the media had tried and convicted me. I thought back to the moment I'd wanted to strike

O'Rourke. Images of me being taken out in cuffs, maybe issued a restraining order, flashed through my mind. How they would have loved that!

Even worse, they maligned Marilyn, our son Brandon, and his wife, Neiani—who were also on my staff. Marilyn's sister, Jennifer, who had been one of my executive assistants, was not safe either. They made public our salaries and repeated the union's claims that they were exorbitant and a risk to the financial health of the local. No one bothered to mention that all were significantly lower than the amounts permitted by the union bylaws. My family members were also paid less than other staff members in the office, despite the fact that they did the lion's share of the work. I had raised my son as my father had raised me—that to work for a union was not a job but a calling—a mission to serve the American worker. Now all he would take away was the bitter realization that labor rewarded loyalty and commitment with slander and destruction.

Others on the staff who were not relatives but part of the "work family" had become so important to me. Leeann Miyamura, my senior executive assistant, had been with the union for twenty-three years when Dias and O'Rourke showed up that morning. She was given less than a minute to decide whether she wanted to be fired or be allowed to retire, and the fact that she chose the latter made it no less painful. Lydia Mahelona, who under the direction of Leeann, Marilyn, and Jennifer handled administrative tasks for the entire office, was also fired. Then there was David Finn and Kris Hoke, our Outer Island representatives. David, the former recording secretary, was a talented young man who to me symbolized what unions *could* be with the right leadership. We not only shared our vision for labor, we articulated it on a regular basis so that it was part of the fabric of our work. Kris Hoke had served as president of Local 1260, but at my request she had stepped down in order to serve as rep. Although it was not required by the bylaws, I had decided it was better to keep staff members and board members separate so they could be objective in doing the local's business. Both Kris and David were also close personal friends with my family and me, and thus became other casualties of May 6.

After spending perhaps the worst Mother's Day in all our years together, Marilyn and I woke up the following Monday to find that our presence had been completely erased from the IBEW website. The logo had been changed, and any pictures that included my family and me had been removed. My YouTube videos, which I had posted as motivational talks to the members, were also gone. The model I had created, a model that had been praised by the same people who were now accusing me of malfeasance—a model I'd hoped and prayed would take labor into a phase of growth and relevance—was being dismantled. Or, as I would later realize, hijacked.

Several other members of the nineteen-person staff were also fired. Within a week, a letter was "accidentally" leaked to media, informing the membership of the Local 1260 of the trusteeship and listing the members who could be "trusted." No one loyal to me was on that list. Those who were, I knew, were the ones who had sold me out.

I sat watching while my name was smeared, not only across the state my family had proudly called home for generations, but across the thousands of union members I considered my brothers and sisters. I could only be grateful that my father wasn't there to witness it.

Somewhere underneath the anger and disbelief, I reminded myself of the credo I had always lived by: do the right thing, and somehow everything will work out. I might not have struck O'Rourke that morning, but I was going to come out swinging.

Chapter 1

In the days that followed, the reasons for my ouster slowly but surely became clear. For years my work—and my outside-the-box approach to labor—had drawn the attention of the IBEW's leadership. Somewhere along the line, this attention had shifted from enthusiasm and admiration to concern that I would campaign to unseat IBEW leadership from office; from then it had only been a matter of time before I had to go. I had seen this many times—threats to the "brotherhood" targeted for termination. But as the saying goes, I truly believed it couldn't happen to me. While this attitude was partially born of naiveté, it was mostly due to my upbringing less than a half hour from the 1260's offices.

By the early 1960s, labor had already passed its prime in America. Not that anyone knew it; in fact, many union enthusiasts wanted to believe it was the beginning of a new era. A few years earlier the American Federation of labor (AFL) had merged with the Congress of Industrial Organizations (CIO), creating an enormous, seemingly indestructible power base. The slight shrinkage in union membership—from 33.2% of American workers in 1955 to 31.4% in 1960—seemed both insignificant and temporary, a lull before labor returned to the levels it enjoyed in its heyday: the Great Depression,

World War II, and Post-War eras. Instead, it would prove to be the beginning of labor's slow, steady march toward irrelevance.

None of this mattered in Pearl City, the rural area on Oahu where I lived with my family. Today, Pearl City is a bustling city complete with Starbucks and a Walmart, but back in the fifties, the area had more sugar cane fields than homes, and one was lucky to find a store open after dark. My parents, Norman and Rowena Ahakuelo, had been born and raised in Honolulu but moved to Pearl City after they married. Their families thought they were crazy for moving "way out there," but all they saw was a safe, close-knit community in which to raise their children. They were also able to buy a home there for just $13,000.

Rowena was of Irish and Hawaiian ancestry; she was also a devout Catholic and strong and protective of her children. On the other hand, she had no problem telling me and my siblings to "get out of the house and don't come back until it gets dark" on days when school was not in session. We got to play, and she got to do her housework without our constant disruptions.

My father ran Local 1260, the same local of the IBEW that I would be removed from decades later. Norman had had a rough time of it growing up; he lost his Chinese-born mother to diabetes when he was just three years old. In the 1930s, his father, Benjamin Ahakuelo, had been one of four Hawaiian men falsely accused of raping Thalia Massie, a well-bred white woman married to Lieutenant Thomas Massie, a naval officer stationed on the island. A bruised and trauma-tized Thalia claimed she had been attacked while walking home from a navy event. When her husband insisted on calling the cops, Thalia gave a license plate number and description of the assailants that led to the arrest of my grandfather and three of his friends, including prize fighter Joseph Kahahawai. However, at trial it came out that on the night of the alleged attack, Kahahawai and the others had been involved in a traffic altercation on the other side of the island. That, coupled with inconsistencies in Thalia Massie's story, led to three weeks of deliberation, a deadlocked jury, and eventually a mistrial. In fact, many on the island were starting to believe that she had not been raped at all. The Massies had a volatile relationship, and it was rumored that her bruises had been inflicted by her husband after he learned she was having an affair with one of his naval buddies.

Enter Grace Hubbard Fortescue, Thalia's mother. It's not clear whether she believed her daughter was attacked and by whom, but she was not willing to wait for another jury to be empaneled. First she hired someone to beat Horace Ida, another of the accused men; then she convinced her son-in-law and two other naval officers to kidnap Joseph Kahahawai, who they tortured and eventually killed.

After that, Honolulu erupted in racial tension. The story soon spread to the mainland, where the press reported on the "anti-white sentiment" that made the island unsafe for Caucasian women. They did not bother to mention that the four men had not been convicted of anything. The situation got so bad that martial law was almost declared. Grace Fortescue, Thomas Massie, and the other two men were arrested for Kahahawai's death, but only because they had been caught red-handed with his body.

That would have been more than enough to put most people away for life, but Fortescue was not most people. Through her connections, she secured the legal representation of famed defense attorney Clarence Darrow. Until then, he had fought for the falsely accused and disenfranchised; now, as a favor to a friend and for the hefty fee of $40,000, he used his name and talent to free a murderer. In the end, Grace and the others were convicted, not of murder, but manslaughter, and the judge, seeking to avoid political fallout, commuted their ten-year sentences to *one hour*, to be served in his office. They then fled to the mainland, where Thalia and Thomas Massie eventually divorced. Thalia later killed herself, whether from the shame of lying or because her marriage and social standing had been destroyed, no one knew. Whatever the case, proving the innocence of the men she had accused became that much harder.

It took years and an investigation by Pinkerton detectives for Ben Ahakuelo and the others to be officially exonerated for the sexual assault. In the meantime, with a fortitude most could not imagine, my grandfather managed to put his life back together. A boxer himself, he developed quite a reputation and even fought a bout at Madison Square Garden. After losing his wife, he remarried and had other children he raised alongside my father. By the time I came along, Ben Ahakuelo was a tough yet caring patriarch who had put past injustices behind him. Still, I'd always wondered what it was like to be suspected of such a horrific crime, and what it was like for my father to grow up in its shadow.

• • •

My childhood could not have been more different, a simple yet happy existence most Americans cannot conceive of today. My parents had little money, and much of what they did have went to Catholic school tuition for me, my two sisters, Aonani and Maile, and three brothers— Kevin, Christian, and Michael. Still, we never felt deprived; quite the opposite. Whether it was the one new pair of shoes we would get that year or the pizza my father brought home for dinner as a special treat, we were grateful for everything we got.

From an early age we were taught that spirituality, personal responsibility, hard work, and education were the keys to living a purpose-driven, successful life. My parents were as strict as they were loving, and my siblings and I had a list of chores—from making our bed to raking leaves—that we had to do each day. Our first priority, however, was our schoolwork. My mother was never so proud as the moment my kindergarten teacher told her I was "going to be someone one day"; she repeated it to me on a regular basis, like a mantra, as if willing it to become a part of me. Mom was also especially devout, and she made me understand from an early age that God was not some abstract concept but a palpable force guiding our everyday lives. My middle name—Francis, after St. Francis of Assisi—and my Hawaiian name—Kahanualoha, or "The Breath of Life"—served as daily reminders of this.

Against this backdrop of spirituality, belief, community, and a strong work ethic, my love of the Labor Movement was born. Some of my earliest memories were of hanging out at the union hall with my father. It seemed there was always something going on there, and whether the men were holding an official meeting or playing a game of cards, their loyalty and camaraderie would be printed indelibly on my mind. Nothing—especially not statistics about union dues, membership rosters, and political cronyism—could undermine that.

Chapter 2

On January 17, 1962, President Kennedy issued an executive order guaranteeing collective bargaining rights to federal employees. The move completely contradicted U.S. policy up to that point. The fear of the havoc a public union could wreak upon society was well-founded. In 1919 the Boston Police Department had unionized and gone on strike. Rioting and looting ensued, until then–Governor Calvin Coolidge put an end to it. But his words would set the tone for decades to follow: "There is no right to strike against the public safety by anybody, anywhere, anytime."

President Woodrow Wilson agreed, calling the strike "an intolerable crime against civilization," as did FDR, who two decades later told the Federation of Federal Employees that "collective bargaining cannot be transplanted into public service." For this reason, Roosevelt, who was a huge proponent of labor, believed that the National Labor Relations Act of 1935 (also known as the Wagner Act) applied only to private sector employees.

Still, Kennedy's decision was deemed a positive one, by both sides of the aisle. On the one hand, it protected workers such as teachers, sanitation workers, hospital workers, and firemen not covered by the Wagner Act; on the other hand, their collective bargaining rights excluded salary increases, which would continue to be set by Congress. It also explicitly forbade public workers from striking. During the 1960s and 70s, Kennedy's decision would bring in tens of thousands of new members and appeared to usher in a new era for the labor movement. Of course, this would later prove to be all smoke and mirrors; unlike private industry, government workers could not be forced to join a union, so 20 to 30 percent of these "members" did not pay dues.

Local 1260 flourished under my father's leadership. He had started his career at Hawaiian Electric, the largest provider in the state, but in 1963, at the age of thirty-two, he went to work for the union. I was just two years old at the time, but by the time I was in grade school, he was running the show. In many ways the structure there mirrored that of our family, meaning he applied the same beliefs and morals with the workers as he did at home. He adhered to the notion that he was his brother's keeper; he felt responsible for the welfare of the members and their families. Similarly, my siblings and I were expected to work hard, support others, and treat people with respect. And above all, we were never, ever to give up. I grew up believing that labor was a positive force for workers and their families, and by extension, the community and the nation.

That's not to say I planned a career in labor. Spirituality governed my younger years, both at home and at school, and for a time I even thought about entering the priesthood. While that notion ended once I discovered girls, my interest in theology continued throughout my education. My parents didn't have much money, but they scrimped and saved in order to send me to Catholic schools—Our Lady of Good Counsel for grade school, and later Maryknoll High School. Each morning I would hop the bus to Honolulu, where Maryknoll was located, in time for early morning mass. This was not required by the school, nor by my parents, and my brothers and sisters did not go to church. I just had an inexplicable need within me to start the day off talking with God and praying that I would live up to His expectations of me. Like most teens, I had choices to make about the kind of people I wanted to associate with—something my parents had taught me would affect the course of my life. Nurturing my faith kept me on track and helped me to choose the "good side of the fence."

As soon as we were old enough, my siblings and I got jobs so we could help our parents with expenses and have some money in our pockets. I worked as an altar boy at funerals and usually made a few dollars in tips. Back then they would lower the casket into the ground at the end of the service. Inevitably, a mourner or two would try to jump in after their loved ones.

"Not now," the priest would tell them. "You'll have your chance."

In 1978, my junior year, I won the St. Thomas Moore Award, which was presented each year to the school's top student in theology. Everyone gathered at a special assembly, where the winner, regardless of grade, was presented with a Bible. It was, for me, a huge honor and reinforced the belief that when one follows one's heart, he will be rewarded.

Maryknoll High School was not just a parochial school, but a competitive college preparatory school. Out of my graduating class of 150 students, 147 of them headed straight to the university. The other three, including myself, joined the military. I, too, had dreams of attending college, preferably on the mainland, but first I had to find a way to pay for it. With four other children to support, there was no way my parents could afford it.

Before I knew it, I was preparing to head off to basic training in South Carolina. While initially my decision to join the army was financial, I soon realized that a sense of purpose drove me. I was about to serve my country, a thought I found exciting. As I would soon learn, this call to duty would add to the foundation already created by my parents and my faith. It would teach me many of the leadership skills I would carry with me throughout my life.

Chapter 3

As I boarded the jumbo 747 for my first flight, I had no idea what to expect. I had never been to the mainland before; I had never even left Hawaii. Nor had I had much contact with people whose backgrounds differed from mine; everyone I knew came from middle-class families and went to parochial schools. As it turned out, my location didn't matter much. We were taken from the plane directly to Fort Jackson, which was a world unto itself, one of barracks and a grueling schedule of running and doing anything else we were ordered to do. Mostly I remember the incessant screaming of the drill sergeant, who clearly thought we did nothing right. This was 1979; the Vietnam War had ended a few years earlier, and several instructors at the camp, including our drill sergeant, had served in it. Although the chances we would be sent into combat were slim, they were preparing us for the possibility, and apparently that sometimes warranted a slap.

Each day, we highly anticipated mail call. We had no cell phones, no emails, and no Internet back then; we were completely cut off from the outside world. At the appointed time we would stand in formation, praying the sergeant would call our names. My mother wrote me quite often, as did some of my friends from high school. I devoured each letter, at once both comforted by news of home and made even lonelier by it. As for my letters, I kept them carefully neutral; I didn't want to upset Mom or anyone else by telling them that our days were spent being yelled at . . . or worse. They wouldn't have understood that, as jarring as it was, I found boot camp quite invigorating. While I couldn't say I enjoyed getting up at the crack of dawn and running for miles, the discipline appealed to me.

As insular as the camp was, its population was the most diverse I had ever known, with men of every race, religion, and background. They were also a tough crowd; in fact, many had been given the choice of the army or prison, although at times it seemed they wished they had made a different decision. Being around them, I had to be tough as well, and I found myself appreciating the way my parents had encouraged me to have a thick skin while growing up.

Whatever our differences, the other men and I soon bonded over lousy meals at the mess and five-mile runs in the blistering heat. Over the next eight weeks these men would become not only my brothers, but my teachers as well. For the first time I realized on a conscious level that a person could be someone to emulate, or they could show me how *not* to be. This lesson would serve me well throughout my life and especially in my career with the union.

Hellish as they were, the weeks of boot camp flew by, then it was off to San Antonio, Texas, for the second leg of my training. When joining the army, we'd had to pick an area in which to specialize, and I had chosen to become a combat medic. The idea of having medical knowledge, coupled with the ability to help people, appealed to me. Compared to basic training, this leg was like being on a three-month vacation. No drill sergeants stood over us screaming, and we spent most of our time in a classroom rather than running around camp. We did have hands-on training, though; first we would be shown a film about how to treat different kinds of wounds, then we would practice on "victims" with fake bullet wounds and bloody gashes. We had to learn how to make split-second decisions to save the lives of our patients and protect ourselves from harm at the same time. I loved every minute of it.

After three months I returned to Hawaii with a newfound purpose: I was going to join the army full time, but not as a medic. I wanted to join the Special Forces. In the meantime, I continued to fulfill my obligation to the Reserves, serving one weekend a month and two weeks in the summer. I also enrolled in Leeward Community College, which was part of the University of Hawaii. Leeward was located in Pearl City, which meant I could live with my parents to save money on room and board. My course of study focused on psychology—not because I planned on a career as a therapist, but because I had always been fascinated by the theories behind human behavior—how to understand people and their motivations for doing things. I had no way of knowing of how well that education would serve me.

To earn money, I also took a part-time job at Hawaiian Electric. Each night I would drive a truck around to the different sites, delivering mail. The work was easy, and although I enjoyed talking to the various employees, rather monotonous. No matter, I told myself, it was only temporary, a way to earn some money until I finished school and joined the army. Before me I saw a life of service to my country and the sort of camaraderie I had enjoyed in basic training. But as the saying goes, if you want to make God laugh, tell Him of your future plans. For while I would indeed have a career serving others, it would come about in quite a different way. It all began with the moment I laid eyes on Marilyn.

Chapter 4

The day I was hired on at Hawaiian Electric was the same day I joined the rank and file of the International Brotherhood of Electrical Workers. Union membership was a condition of employment—the result of a union security clause put in place years earlier. But even if I'd had a choice, I would have joined the union anyway. At that time the IBEW had a vision and direction—namely, to serve as a necessary intermediary between workers and employers for the benefit of both. Besides, my father was head of Local 1260, and to not show my support would have been unthinkable.

On a larger scale, labor in America was in the grips of one its more obvious existential crises. The years 1979 to 1984 saw more union mergers than any other period since the formation of the AFL-CIO in 1955. Union leaders liked to point to the clause in the AFL-CIO's constitution that labor organizations should join together in order to consolidate their power and do away with competition over jurisdictions, but the truth was that many of these organizations were struggling fiscally.

A 1977 Supreme Court case, *Abood v. Detroit Board of Education*, indicated that the political winds were starting to change with regard to labor. Michigan State law allowed union shops within public sector workplaces, and for the previous ten years the Detroit Federation of Teachers had been the only union for that city's schoolteachers. One of those teachers, D. Louis Abood, objected to being forced to join the union, particularly because his dues were being used in support of political candidates favored by its leadership. The Supreme Court held, on First Amendment grounds, that public workers could not be compelled to finance positions and activities they did not agree with. On the other hand, the court knew if it made all dues optional, it would likely put unions out of business, so they held that members still had to pay expenses—or "agency fees"—related to collective bargaining. The decision was seen as a balance between pro and anti-labor sentiments, but it would leave the door open for other cases later on.

By 1979, union members comprised only 24 percent of the American workforce, a significant decrease from 35% in the mid-1940s. This was in part due to state laws enacted subsequent to Abood that allowed public employees to engage in collective bargaining without officially unionizing (and without paying dues); in other cases, changes in a particular industry or economic conditions led to reduced ranks. Most of the mergers in the late 70s and early 80s therefore involved larger organizations absorbing smaller ones, with the latter often experiencing significant changes to their bylaws and even their constitutions; it all depended on lengthy and often secret negotiations conducted by management. Smaller organizations often "shopped around" for the best offer. For example, in December of 1980, the Oregon Service Employees agreed to join the Service Employees

International, one of the largest AFL-CIO affiliates, only after they were promised that they would never be put under trusteeship.

Oftentimes the rank and file knew little about what was being discussed behind closed doors; this was how a federal judge ruled when in February of 1984, the Telecommunications International Union considered a merger with several larger unions, including the IBEW. The Telecommunications International distributed additional information to its members, but by then leadership had officially endorsed the American Federal of State, County and Municipal Employees (AFSCME).

None of this was on my mind, however, when I took that job at Hawaiian Electric; I always viewed it as a stepping-stone to something else. And indeed, that's exactly what it turned out to be, and in more ways than one.

Each day, after leaving class, I'd head over to Hawaiian Electric for my three thirty to eight p.m. shift. I'd drive around to the various plants, chitchatting with whomever happened to be collecting the mail that day. My favorite person, though, was a woman named Gloria Mindoro, who worked part time as a security guard at the Waiau Plant. While I generally liked most people I met, Gloria and I became fast friends. On nights I knew she was working, I'd stop somewhere along my route and pick up dinner for the both of us. She also worked in the cafeteria at a public school; like me, she too had taken a part-time job at Hawaiian Electric to pay for an education, but not for herself. She and her husband Edward had three daughters—Corrine was my age, and their youngest, Jennifer, still attended a costly Catholic high school. Their middle daughter was seventeen-year-old Marilyn.

Edward, who worked as a stevedore on the docks, was also a rank-and-file union member. After his shift he'd often drive to the parking lot and catch some shuteye while he waited for Gloria to punch out. Other times, he'd join in the conversation, and I found him as warm and engaging as his wife.

In the fall of 1980, I had decided to take a full-time position at Hawaiian Electric. I mentioned this to Gloria and asked if she knew anyone who would like to take over my route.

"Actually, I do," she replied. "That shift would be a perfect fit with Marilyn's school schedule."

I told her I would put in a good word, and we left it at that. Then, one November night, a car pulled up as Gloria and I were chatting. Thinking it was Edward, I turned to say hello and was instead greeted by the sight of the most beautiful girl I'd ever seen sitting behind the wheel. I glanced back at Gloria and asked, "Is that your daughter?"

She nodded. "Yes, that is Marilyn."

When I looked at the young woman again, she stared back at me. We exchanged shy smiles, then I said to Gloria, "Why don't you give me your phone number so I can call and help her through the application . . ."

The offer of assistance, while sincere, also had another purpose—I was determined to ask Marilyn out. I had no reason to play it cool. How many young men could say they became friends with a girl's parents before courting her? I knew I was in with Gloria and Edward;

now I just had to see how receptive Marilyn was to the idea. I sweetened the pot by planning the best evening I could think of—tickets to the Lionel Ritchie and the Commodores concert, which at the time was quite a big deal. She agreed, and by the end of the night, I knew the good time we'd had had nothing to do with the music. I was in love.

On July 18, 1981, eight months after we met, Marilyn and I were married. Some people may have thought we rushed things, especially since we were so young, but I didn't see the point in waiting. I knew in my bones that I wanted to spend the rest of my life with her. As we stood before Father Terrance Watanabe, a young priest just out of the seminary, I realized that everything about that day supported my decision. The church, Our Lady of Good Counsel, was one my maternal grandfather had helped build. As a child I had attended mass and grammar school there. I had even helped build the stone wall surrounding the building. It had taught me what it was like to build something from the ground up. The church was part of my spiritual foundation, and now it would become part of the foundation to my marriage to Marilyn.

Chapter 5

As Marilyn and I were just starting to build our new life together, the foundation of American labor was about to be dealt a critical blow. On August 5, 1981, the Professional Air Traffic Controllers Organization (PATCO) walked off the job after the FAA refused to give in to their demands for higher pay and a shorter work week. A showdown between them and President Ronald Reagan ensued. After pointing out that they were in violation of the clause of the Taft-Hartley Act that made it illegal for federal employees to strike, the president told them they had forty-eight hours to return to work. Just 1,300 air traffic controllers complied, and Reagan not only fired the other 11,345 but banned them from federal service for life. It was, as U.S. labor historian Joseph A. McCartin wrote, "One of the most important events in late twentieth century U.S. labor history."

It wasn't the first time PATCO had wreaked havoc upon the aviation industry. Founded in 1968 by famous attorney and pilot F. Lee Bailey, it had begun as a professional organization but was reclassified as a trade union the following year by the U.S. Civil Service Commission. Over the years they had caused several disruptions in air travel, including so-called "sick-outs," in which many air traffic controllers would call out sick in order to circumvent the law against strikes. Why they officially struck this time was unclear; perhaps it was because PATCO, which was disillusioned with the Carter administration, had backed Reagan for president. He in turn had appeared to sympathize with their struggles; of course, that sympathy did not extend to trampling on federal law and crippling air travel across the United States.

I watched the situation unfold along with the rest of the country, unable to believe what I was seeing. It wasn't the strike that shocked me so much—throughout its history labor had held entire industries and even the public for ransom. I had never agreed with that approach, instead favoring arm's-length negotiations between workers and employers, and I didn't now. I wasn't surprised by Reagan's hard stance, either. After all, when you play chicken, you always run the risk that your opponent won't blink. No, what stunned me was the lack of support other unions showed PATCO. Labor, I had always believed, was a brotherhood, a movement of solidarity to protect all American workers. Their refusal to stand by their "brothers" now broke the back of labor as much as anything Reagan did. The president's actions showed employers that they needn't be held hostage by striking employees; they could simply replace them. The strike, wielded with such might for more than a century, had lost much of it teeth, and unions would never again approach the bargaining table with the same confidence. Reagan's move against PATCO, coupled with the deregulation policies of his administration, heralded in an era of "give back" contracts—those in which unions made concessions rather than demanding raises in pay and benefits.

The recession at that time also hit labor hard, particularly the steel and auto workers. When some suggested that high union wages were at least in part to blame for the inflation, United Auto Workers President Owen Bieber replied, "Hogwash." Thinking a different president might swing things in their favor, labor leaders threw their support behind Walter Mondale's unsuccessful 1984 campaign.

• • •

The PATCO incident, while disconcerting, meant little to me at the time. Local 1260 was still making a positive difference in workers' lives—negotiating contracts, promoting favorable working conditions, and ensuring that those injured on the job received workman's compensation. Shortly after our marriage, Marilyn and I moved to Hilo, on the Big Island, where homes were less expensive and Hawaiian Electric paid nine dollars an hour instead of seven. I took another shift position, this time as a meter reader.

Even with the increase, money was tight. Marilyn made minimum wage—just $4 an hour in 1983—at the office supply company where she worked, and thanks to a high interest rate, we had a thousand-dollar-a-month mortgage. We made it work, though, and a few years later started our family, welcoming our son Brandon into the world in 1983, and our daughter Megan in 1985. It was the most joyous time in our lives, and supporting them was my sole focus. But while I may not have given much conscious thought to my career trajectory,

I always had this sense of a mission, that something bigger was out there for me.

At first, I did not take an active part in the union, aside from the occasional membership meeting with my father. I still loved the camaraderie I had witnessed as a kid; I also enjoyed being able to observe the relationship between the union and the company from both sides. Eventually, I was appointed the shop steward, or point person, on the job site. I now had my first taste of serving as liaison between employer and employee, and found I thoroughly enjoyed it. I also realized that contrary to what the majority of union members believed, most employers were not out to abuse their workers; they were simply trying to preserve their business interests.

The same year my daughter was born, I also got my first taste of the hypocrisy that ran rampant throughout labor (and in direct contradiction to its official political message) when I attended an IBEW conference in San Antonio with my father.

We had no sooner checked into the hotel when my father shepherded me back out to the rental car for an exploratory mission. Dad didn't travel often, but wherever he went he made sure to locate two places: a Catholic church and a Chinese restaurant. He drew strength from going to Mass, and he was not about to miss it because it was inconvenient. He could be standing around a craps table in a smoked-filled Vegas casino and he'd announce to the other men, "Okay, Mass is at six p.m. Anyone who is coming with me, be outside by five thirty."

Finding a Chinese restaurant—especially a decent one—presented more of a challenge. Sure, it was easy in big cities like San Francisco and New York, but San Antonio in the eighties? I often wondered why my father, who was half Chinese and had grown up eating authentic Chinese cooking, would subject himself to the slop he found in some of these places, but he insisted. When he was dissatisfied with the meal, he'd argue with the waiters, but I could tell he enjoyed every minute of it. It was all part of the ritual. In years to come, I too would attend Mass whenever I travelled; it reminded me of the many blessings God had bestowed upon me, and it strengthened and sustained me in times of stress. When it came to Chinese restaurants, however, I was a bit more discriminating than Dad.

The conference was packed with members from all over the country, including some from the International in Washington, DC. They were overwhelmingly white, Irish, and many years—sometimes even decades—older than me. While I was not surprised by the age difference (a saying in the IBEW said that "your career doesn't start until age sixty-five"), I did take note of the lack of ethnic diversity, especially when I overheard one of the men say, "There's a place for people *like that* in the union" and knew without a doubt that he was referring to people of color. Sure, they were allowed in the union, but only as rank and file. No people of color, and certainly no women, held any leadership positions. My father was not surprised; he had seen much of the same while in the army, both at Ft. Dix, New Jersey, and in Korea, and the experience had seemed to cement his belief that his place was in Hawaii. For me, though, I got a rather startling glimpse behind the curtain that was the labor movement, and the first of many wake-up calls I would get over the years.

So even though union members were quite jovial and welcoming to the contingency from Local 1260—"Hey, it's the guys from Hawaii!"—I always remembered one of my father's favorite sayings: "Beware of white men bearing gifts."

• • •

Marilyn and I might have settled permanently on the Big Island had Brandon not been diagnosed with asthma. The frequent eruptions of the volcano on the Big Island exacerbated his condition, so much so that in 1989 we decided to sell our home and move back to Oahu. We bought a home ten miles from my parents, and I resumed my shift work at Hawaiian Electric as an equipment operator, which meant I managed the equipment on the first three floors of the building. The process involved burning fossil fuels to make electricity, and my role was to essentially "make water" using an evaporator package. I needed knowledge of how to introduce the right chemicals in the correct proportion to steam.

I also came to this job armed with new experience. A few years earlier, I had been elected to my first office within the IBEW, as vice chairman of my unit. Then later, in 1987, I was elected to serve on the Executive Board. Unlike the unit position, the Executive Board position was a statewide one, with members from every company on each of the islands voting by mail ballot. Winning this election was both exciting and a bit surprising, especially since I had not really run a campaign per se. I had simply listed my name in the newsletter as a contender, then made a few phone calls to people I knew and mentioned I was running. I was just twenty-six years old, running against men nearly twice my age and veterans of the union.

I held these positions in addition to my regular work, and while they were unpaid, they provided a wealth of opportunities to observe various situations, both among the workers, and between the workers and their employer. In each situation, I learned to take note of the needs of the parties and the value of bridging the gap between these needs. I simultaneously learned confidence and the need to leave the ego out of such negotiations, and to approach them calmly and with respect for the positions of all parties. Of the many things I had learned from my father was the art of winning over the members. This was not always easy, given my age and relative inexperience. While I was mostly treated with respect, a couple of men took the attitude that I was a "kid" who knew nothing. This only confirmed another thing I had learned from my father: respect is gained over time and as a result of one's actions, not from the title on his or her business card.

Back on Oahu, I resumed work at the Hawaiian Electric plant, while Marilyn settled into her new role as administrative assistant to the general manager of a local television station. There, she learned about the industry from the ground up, including how to run a successful media campaign. She also made countless contacts in the entertainment community since television stations were unionized as well. Her work would take her on a completely different professional course, yet one that would eventually align with my own.

Chapter 6

I was not surprised when my father asked me to leave Hawaiian Electric and come to work at Local 1260. However, I did recognize it as the proverbial fork in the road. By that time I had already been at Hawaiian Electric for eleven years; I knew what was expected of me and what I could expect from the company. I also knew that if I wanted to, I could rise through the ranks of management and probably live a comfortable life. But would this be enough? When I envisioned the years ahead, I knew the answer was no. In my brief time as an active union member, I had tasted the satisfaction and sense of accomplishment that came from liaising between the workers and the company, for the benefit of both. At that point, I still believed that the best way to accomplish this was by working on the union side, and so on February 17, 1992, at the age of thirty-one, I became a full-time employee of the IBEW.

Now, under my father's direct tutelage, I was able to take my "education" to the next level. Each day I learned something new about negotiating contracts and addressing the needs of workers and companies alike; moreover, I learned each day how much I *didn't* know.

Dad had always been a man of simple but profound philosophies, all of which centered around integrity and respect. "Always be true to yourself," he said, "and to what you are trying to accomplish." When I first joined the team, he handed me a small handbook entitled "Tact" and suggested I allow it to guide me in all of my dealings with others. Our goal was not to be locked in combat with companies, but to build long-term relationships with them. Of course that was not to say all employers would feel that way, but in his opinion, 90 percent of companies would work with me.

Before long, I got the chance to put his advice to the test. In my role as business representative I was assigned three companies—Maui Electric, Chevron Refinery, and Kauai Island Utility Co-op. One day I got a call from the president of Maui Electric, who without preamble said the words I would hear all too often in my career in labor.

"Brian, we got a serious problem."

"Okay . . . ," I said as several scenarios ran through my mind; none of them, however, were as strange as the truth. Apparently, the entire line crew—twenty men in total—had decided to bring their firearms to work. They hid them in the utility truck, which they then drove to the mountains and began shooting off live rounds. When someone—it wasn't clear who—called the company to report them, the men were promptly fired by their department manager. The company was now left with a skeleton crew of about ten men; this was the "serious problem" the president had referred to when he called me.

After assuring him that I would take care of it, I sought my father's counsel. His answer, although typical of him, was a bit surprising given the severity of the situation.

"I want you to resolve this," he said.

From my first day at the union, my father made it clear that he expected me to resolve my own cases. At first I thought he was nuts. I knew he'd always been in favor of resolving issues on our own, rather than rushing into arbitration, which would cost the union money; however, I also knew for a fact that other reps sent their cases to arbitration all the time. It seemed to me that Dad was simply trying to show everyone that I wouldn't be getting any special treatment.

In my opinion, if any situation called for third-party intervention, it was the one at Maui Electric, but Dad wouldn't hear of it. The flight from Oahu to Maui is twenty-five minutes, and I spent it wondering what God was trying to teach me. Perhaps He just wanted me to get out of this business altogether.

The first thing I did when I arrived was meet with the men and read them the riot act. "What the hell were you thinking?"

The men looked at each other, then at me, but offered no answer. What could they say that could possibly justify shooting live rounds on state land—an act that was not only in violation of company policy but the law as well? Finally I told them to go on home and I would be in touch.

My next visit was to the president of the company. He was cordial enough, but his mind appeared to be made up. The men had to go.

"This easy thing," I began, "would be to fire everyone. The hardest thing would be for you and me to sit down and figure out how to bring everyone back . . ."

He raised an eyebrow at me.

". . . and then they would serve as a lesson to the other employees and advocates for good behavior."

The president looked at me for a moment, then nodded. By the end of the meeting, all twenty men had their jobs back. Not until I left his office, utterly exhilarated, did I realize why my father had been so tough on me. He was forcing me to develop my own conflict resolution skills, rather than rely on another layer of bureaucracy to fix things. As a result, I learned how to keep someone employed, as in the case of the twenty linemen, or if they were fired, to at least collect severance. It was all a balancing act.

Of all the things my father taught me about unions and about life, this was one of the greatest blessings. His teachings would make me a better leader, not only in my current position but in the years to come.

• • •

As much as I enjoyed being a business representative, I soon found myself drawn to the organizing side of the union business. I couldn't imagine anything more exciting than going before a group of disenfranchised workers and inspiring them to believe in a better way.

For guidance, I turned to Hank Reeves, who spearheaded Local 1260's organizing efforts. In my downtime, I began to shadow him and was immediately impressed with the way he spoke to people. Hank taught me the laws about organizing, including what you can and cannot say to workers. He also showed me the subtle nuances— namely, when you should say something and when you shouldn't. Like all excellent teachers, he was also willing to let me fall on my face. When one day I told him I wanted to meet with a group of prospective members, he did not try to deter me. Indeed, I did experience some early failures, and they served as my most valuable lesson of all: I learned that failure, when viewed from the proper perspective, is a key ingredient of success, for in failure we learn to evaluate, and if necessary, reinvent ourselves.

Chapter 7

The late 1990s were a time of unprecedented scandal within labor, and while these incidents took place in New York City, they tarnished the reputation of unions throughout the country. In 1996, AFL-CIO leaders pled guilty to extorting one million dollars in bribes known as "sweetheart contracts." In June of 1997, two members of the Lucchese crime family pled guilty to murdering a mob rival who also happened to be the head of a local painter's union. That year, the president of the transit union in New York City was also convicted of taking kickbacks. And in February of 1998, the head of the New York City Janitors Union was ousted for his outrageous fiscal abuses, including a $450,000 salary and a penthouse in Manhattan. The fallout was only exacerbated by the fact that he was given a $1.5 million severance check. Between the years 1996 and 1998, locals in New York representing three hundred thousand workers were placed under trusteeship for a host of crimes, fiscal and otherwise.

While nothing of this magnitude happened at the IBEW—and certainly not at Local 1260—I, too, was beginning to see the unpleasant side of labor. In 1996, Mike Lucas, the IBEW's director of organizing, was rather abruptly terminated from the union. For years, Lucas had been considered a rising star within the IBEW, not only because of his hard work but because he had excellent ideas for taking labor into the next century. I could attest to this, for I had met Lucas that year at a conference for which I had served as a delegate. Like me, he was passionate in his beliefs that everything in labor must done in support of the American worker, and that in supporting the American worker, we were supporting America itself. So what had he done that warranted being fired? I wasn't sure, but the firing coincidentally happened shortly after he made known his intention to run for president of the union. No one said it outright, but the implication was clear: Lucas had become a threat to someone and had to go. It wasn't the first time I had heard of such shady dealings, but it was the first I had seen it happen to someone on such a large scale and who would have been a positive force within the IBEW. But I refused to let such things poison me. I still believed, deeply, that I had a role to play in advocating for workers, and perhaps even stopping such injustices within the union from happening.

I had a lot to learn.

• • •

When my father retired in 1997, many assumed that I would take over as Local 1260's business manager. For precisely this reason, he instead offered the position to a union veteran named Harry, with the understanding that he would serve for three years then hand the reigns over to me. Harry would later renege on the deal, but it never occurred to me to run against him. Growing up in the union, I had learned a respect for its rules—official and unofficial—one of which was you wait your turn and you always, always leave the dance with the one who brought you. Although technically Harry hadn't brought me anywhere, I remained loyal to the process. Besides, Harry's continued presence didn't affect my job much. He had never been all that interested in the actual work—oftentimes he didn't even show up to the office—so I got to learn the ropes without always feeling like I was in a fishbowl. And learn I did, often on the fly, while sitting across the negotiating table from employers as we went line by line over a contract.

Even before coming to the union, I had gotten my feet wet with regard to contracts; I witnessed two negotiations back in 1990. But during a major negotiation with Hawaiian Electric in 1992 I really got perspective on—and fell in love with—the process. My most valuable lessons, however, had less to do with legalese and everything to do with dealing with people. Coming up in the union clubhouse, I had heard much about the "big, bad companies" that sought to take advantage of the little guy. Since going to work for Local 1260, I had come to realize that the vast majority of employers were not "evil"; they were just simply trying to do business. What it took to do this depended on a myriad of ever-changing variables, from economic and environmental concerns to geopolitical situations half a world away.

In addition, federal and state laws had become more protective of workers' rights over the years: for example, the Occupational Safety and Health Act (OSHA) signed into law by President Nixon in 1970.

OSHA created an administration and an agency, both of which were charged with making sure companies adhered to certain standards with regard to hazardous chemicals, and penalties when they violated those standards. It was one of the many rights that in the past had been fought for workers' respective unions. Indeed, it was a reason that so many workers wanted to unionize in the first place.

With those protections in place, the union-employer relationship had evolved, or at least it should have. My father knew this. He had changed throughout his career, going from the more adversarial banging-your-fist-on-the-table style historically embraced by labor, to one of relationship building. He'd learned over the years that this was the way to get what he wanted. Still, he did like to put on a show in front of the members so they didn't think he'd gone "soft."

Retired or not, Dad remained my close advisor and confidante. We would discuss everything from specific goals on our professional bucket lists to the future of labor itself.

That didn't mean we always agreed. Oftentimes, he didn't disagree with my ideas per se; he just thought they would never happen. He thought I was crazy when I told him I was going to get drug coverage for retired Hawaiian Electric employees; he'd pushed for this for thirty-four years, with no success. Undeterred, I met with the company and managed to negotiate a choice. Retirees could choose between vision/dental coverage and their prescription meds, depending on their needs.

In 1998, I met with Hawaiian Electric on another critical issue: workers' recalculated pension. I knew that rather than getting it in increments, some people wanted to take a lump sum that they could use to pay off their home, send their kids to college, or whatever else they wanted. In short, they wanted control of their own money. Hawaiian Electric had always been vehemently opposed to this; however, when I explained to them that the ideally fully complied with the Employee Retirement Income Security Act (ERISA) and would not cost the company any money, they gave in, to the tune of $50,000 per member.

Brokering deals like this made me realize that bridging the gap between these two parties had become the best way to serve members. It was not just my job; it had become my calling.

• • •

Shortly after my father's retirement, I heard of an A-76 study being conducted at the U.S. naval base on Guam. The military conducts this type of study in order to determine whether it is economically and logistically prudent to privatize the work.

In the case of Guam, it apparently was, for in 1999, the U.S. Navy awarded the contract to Raytheon, a major military contractor. The company would hire about a thousand civilians to work at the base. Although Guam was not in Local 1260's jurisdiction—in fact, the IBEW did not have a presence there at all—the news piqued my interest. About one thousand Raytheon employees were to work at the base—nonunion employees who might need representation. Still,

I didn't go down there right away. I figured a few years should be enough time for Raytheon to show its true colors. If their intention was to screw over the workers, I would step in. Sure enough, by December of 2001, I got a call from one of Raytheon's employees; the company was planning huge wage cuts that would severely impact its workers' quality of life.

This was not completely an altruistic move, however. Over the past few years Local 1260 had taken a real hit, both in terms of membership and money. The reduced ranks, which had much to do with the economic climate at the time, meant less dues coming in, and Harry had done nothing to stem the bleeding, let alone turn things around. By 2001, we had just $80,000 in the general treasury, and if we wanted to remain solvent, we needed to bring in revenue, and quickly.

The IBEW had no presence in Guam at the time. I decided to go down there and meet with the employees to see how I could help. There I was, 3,300 miles from home, alone and with limited resources.

It was a true David and Goliath situation. Founded in 1922 in Cambridge, Massachusetts, Raytheon had played critical roles in national defense for more than half a century—from the radar defense it provided to the navy during World War II to its Patriot Missile that took down Iraqi scuds during the Persian Gulf War. They had high-powered attorneys and human resources from their corporate offices in Boston—the type that didn't break a sweat, despite wearing pricey three-piece suits in Guam.

I was alone, nearly four thousand miles from home, and operating on a shoestring budget. The rule of thumb for organizing is one organizer for every hundred workers. Since we had neither the money nor the manpower for that, I had to find more creative ways to launch a campaign. The first step was to place an ad in the local paper, letting the locals know the IBEW was in town to serve the needs of the workers. Next, I filed a petition with the National Labor Relations Board (NLRB). They would send representatives down to Guam at the end of January, at which time Raytheon's workers would vote on whether they wanted to join the union or not. The Volunteer Organizing Committee (VOC) I had recruited would serve as my only "staff."

The company countered with a full-fledged campaign, including Twenty-five Reasons Not to Join the Union. Each day, they broadcasted a new reason that I and the VOC would have to overcome.

One day, a VOC member called to tell me that the Raytheon people had invited them all to a golf outing!

"What do we do, Brian?" he asked, managing to convey both a desire to go and guilt for even bringing it up.

I thought about it for a moment. "Go ahead," I told him. "Enjoy yourself, then come back and we'll continue our work."

"Really?"

"Yeah. If you want to play golf, play golf."

This accomplished two things—it allowed my guys, who had been working nonstop on the campaign, to blow off some steam; it also signaled to the bigshots at the company that we were not intimidated or impressed by them. Of course, we experienced plenty of moments when we were both intimidated and impressed, but I refused to let doubt seep into my mind and heart. I just focused on my number-one reason for being there: I truly believed unionization would make a critical difference in the lives of the workers.

Over the next month I made friends with everyone. After working all day I would crawl into bed, exhausted, only to have sleep elude me. I'd take a few laps around the hotel's corridors, chatting with the housekeeping staff or whoever happened to be working the concierge desk.

The hardest part was not knowing whether I was winning. Sure, in the moment the workers responded to us, but I had no illusions. The company was playing hardball, and I had no idea what the verdict would be. The only thing I could do was keep moving forward. Finally, the day of the vote arrived. I walked into the room cognizant that the chips were stacked against me but confident that I had done all I could. As the NLRB began to count the ballots, however, it looked as though our efforts had not been enough. When the first seventy votes were no, I looked around the room and thought, *I don't believe this—I came down here for nothing. I've spent over a month away from my family for nothing.*

The seventy-first vote was a yes, but by that time it sounded like a cruel joke. But then came another yes, and another. Oddly enough, the ensuing back and forth between yeses and nos was almost more painful. The room was silent as a tomb.

When the final tally came, the workers had voted 398 to 350 to join the IBEW. The room erupted into cheers, and the company representatives came over and shook my hand, but I was so overwhelmed with pride that it barely registered. It wasn't only proud of myself, for although I had devoted every ounce of my energy to the effort, I hadn't done it alone. The credit also went to the VOC and, most of all, the workers. All I had really done was to help them believe in themselves.

Guam turned out to be a victory for everyone involved. Subsequent negotiations resulted in a contract that benefitted both the workers and the company, which made me as proud as the win itself. The deal also took Local 1260 out of danger. The new members brought our roster up from 1,985 to 3,003; it also brought in an additional $300,000 a year in dues. It would turn out to be the largest single organizing win in IBEW history. When I got back to Local 1260, the phone was running off the hook. Guam had put me on the map, and eventually led to a target on my back.

Chapter 8

Many local unions, at least at the IBEW, enjoyed such a large degree of day-to-day autonomy that it was easy to forget that they were under the purview, not only of the International but the AFL-CIO as well. Given our location on Hawaii, this feeling was perhaps even more pronounced at Local 1260. While we were aware that we were part of a larger movement, our immediate mission was to serve our members. Occasionally, though, we'd be reminded of the vast machinery pulling the strings from the mainland.

When in December of 2003 I was invited to go to a class in the Washington, DC, area, I knew it was more of an order than a request. While there, I and the other attendees would be evaluated on our organizing skills by none other than the director of organizing for *all* unions under the AFL-CIO umbrella. In the world of labor, this man was close to the top of the food chain.

Still, as I filed into the classroom at the George Meany Center for Labor Studies, I found I was looking forward to the class. Over the years I had learned that while locals around the country had issues unique to their respective regions and political climates, they had common challenges as well. Powwowing with other union leaders would be an excellent opportunity to swap valuable experiences and knowledge.

After speaking for twenty-five minutes or so, the director posed a question to the class: What would we do to organize people we didn't know, in a place that was unfamiliar to us? Several hands went up, and his gaze flicked over them before landing on mine.

"Well," I said when he nodded at me, "the first thing I would do is put an ad in the local paper to announce that the union is in town and when we'd be holding our meetings."

The words were barely out of my mouth when the director shook his head. "That will never work."

But it already has worked, I wanted to say, taken aback by his dismissive attitude. Instead, I held my tongue. Other muckety-mucks— including the sitting president of the IBEW—were in attendance, and it seemed they too were sizing us up, although to what end I wasn't sure. Whatever the case, I didn't feel like making an issue of it. But when I later brought up another idea only to be shot down again, I decided enough was enough. I had come to the class anticipating, if not a passionate discussion then at least a useful exchange of information, but apparently that was not to be.

As I explained that my methods were not only possible but had a proven track record, I could tell the director was waiting for the opportunity to tell me all the reasons I didn't know what I was talking about. Then I mentioned Guam. By that time, my organizing win on the island had spread like wildfire through the IBEW; it had even reached the ears of some at the AFL-CIO. I could tell the director was not pleased at being corrected in front of a group of people—a feeling later confirmed by the abysmal evaluation he gave me. The whole experience was an eye-opener. Clearly, he was punishing me for taking him down a peg, but more importantly, it revealed that in labor, egos, not the interests of the workers, may be the true "mission."

• • •

Apparently my subpar evaluation did not greatly concern the International, because a few months later they offered me the position of International representative—specifically, the organizing coordinator—for the IBEW's 9th District. By any standards, being an International rep was a plumb assignment. I would also essentially be my own boss, working from home and without anyone looking over my shoulder. It was also well paid and secure; if I wanted, I could have remained in that position until I retired. But more than that, I had an opportunity to facilitate the organizing efforts of locals in the westernmost states, including Hawaii.

Although I accepted the job, I did so with a heavy heart. My beloved father had been diagnosed with late-stage liver cancer and did not have long to live. The job, which involved regular travel among approximately sixty locals, required me to move to Nevada. During one of our heart-to-heart talks, he made his wishes quite clear: he wanted to die at home; he wanted his funeral to be a small, intimate gathering; and he wanted to be cremated and his ashes buried at the military cemetery so, as a veteran of the Korean War, he would "get what the government owed him." Finally, he insisted that I take this next step in my career, even though it meant it would take me away from home. With his blessing, I agreed to go.

It was the first time, other than the army, that I'd be living on the mainland. The union made the transition as smooth as possible, putting me and my family up in a hotel until we could get settled. For the next two months we explored the area and finally decided on a house right off the Vegas strip. We also discovered a large Hawaiian community, which was helpful as we acclimated to our new environment.

Everything seemed to be falling into place for my kids as well. After serving two tours in the Middle East, Brandon had decided to follow in my footsteps. He returned to the States in 2004 and moved to San Diego, where he worked for Local 465 as an organizer. As my father had mentored me, I tried to impart some of my knowledge to my son. While he mostly agreed with me philosophically, he was definitely a product of his generation when it came to style. He also argued with me much more than I had with my father, which I alternately found annoying and amusing. When the business manager of Local 465 died of pancreatic cancer, Brandon decided it was time for a change—he wanted to be close to his family and get a "regular" job. He moved to Vegas and took a job at Nevada Power, but he remained a member of the IBEW—now at Local 396—and even served as shop steward. It seemed the union was in our blood.

Brandon also shared my ability to acclimate quickly to new situations and environments. Of the many friends he made at his job, Eric was the closest. Like Brandon, Eric was into physical fitness, and the two would often get together at Eric's house to lift weights or punch the bag. Brandon's career choice turned out to be fortuitous for his sister, too. Just as I had met Marilyn through her mother years earlier, Brandon introduced Megan to Eric. The two would eventually marry.

Brandon also met his future wife in Vegas. Like us, Neiani was a transplant from Hawaii, and happened to be attending the same graduation party. The connection was instant, and they soon married as well. Before we knew it, both of our children had also purchased their own homes, leaving Marilyn and me with a large, empty house. It was surreal to think of all the time that had passed in the blink of an eye, but any sadness we felt was far outweighed by the gratitude that our Brandon and Megan had met such wonderful spouses. Our family was truly blessed.

After a brief orientation in Sacramento, California, I was ready to hit the ground running. I was also more grateful than ever that I would be running my own show. Of the fifteen people on the district staff, I was the only one issued a computer. In 2003, this was another red flag—an indicator that the union was unwilling to adopt the practices of the times or, even worse, was woefully unaware of them.

On May 4, barely a month after I left Hawaii, my father quietly slipped away. As I boarded the flight to Hawaii, my one consolation was that he had died at home, surrounded by my mother, my brothers and sisters and their children, as well as my own son and daughter. It had taken some doing on my part to see that this wish was honored, as my siblings had felt rather strongly that he remain in the hospital until the end. I did ignore one of his wishes, though, and that was his desire for a small funeral. My father was a well-known fixture on Oahu, and I wanted to him to be paid the homage he so richly deserved.

As supportive as he was, my father did have mixed feelings about my becoming an International rep, as he believed the people were much more callous on the mainland, both in a general sense and especially within the labor movement.

It wasn't long before I realized that he'd been right once again. I saw other reps go after the locals, screaming at them, sometimes over a legitimate issue but oftentimes just to let them know who was "in charge"; this, despite the fact that the International reps were not bosses at all, but representatives, there to facilitate the work with employers on behalf of the union members. Many on the mainland seemed to be more concerned with climbing the ladder. They wanted to "be something" yet didn't seem to have any idea what that something was.

On the other hand, I loved every minute of the work. Most of my time was spent traveling from local to local, addressing grievances and providing support around organizing. I would talk to staff about the ingredients of a successful organizing campaign so we could educate workers about the benefits of labor. Each local was like a unique family—some functional, some dysfunctional, and it was challenging and fulfilling to adapt my style to each, and forge rich relationships in the process.

I also realized the gaps in communication between the locals and the IBEW, and while I still considered myself an advocate for locals and their independence, it was strange to realize that the staff members often saw me as an "International guy."

Once, after receiving a call from the Local 11 in Los Angeles, I flew there to see how I could help. When the staff member picked me up from the airport, he admitted his surprise. "The International never follows up," he said. "They never come when we tell them our problems."

For me, though, the only real problem was a lack of inspiration. When I addressed the membership, I didn't just talk at them, I tried to lay the foundation and inspire them. When you believe in yourself, there is always a better day for yourself and your family.

For the next two years or so, I relieved a constant stream of emails and phone calls from locals, asking for my help. But another phone call from Washington, DC, would once again shift the trajectory of my life.

"Brian, we want you to come to DC."

At first, when the caller said he was Ed Hill, I was completely shocked. Sure, I had just attended the 2006 convention in Cleveland, Ohio, but why would the president of the IBEW be calling me? Assuming he was asking me to attend another meeting, I said, "Sounds good. When do you want me there?"

Hill laughed. "No, I don't think you get it. I want you to come out and be the director of industrial organizing."

I stared at my phone for a minute, wondering if it was a hoax. Then I thought perhaps he had called me by mistake. He was asking me to be a key player in the Washington, DC, headquarters!

"Are you sure you got the right Brian?" I asked, unable to believe it. "I'll need a couple of days to think about it."

"Okay," he laughed jovially, "go talk it over with your wife and let me know."

Although Marilyn and I did discuss it, it was only to confirm that we were indeed going to accept. An opportunity to influence union organizing on that level was too good to pass up.

On October 31, 2006, I flew across the country to DC. I've never been a big proponent of coincidences; in fact, I've always been a firm believer that everything happens for a reason. The fact that it was Halloween should have come as no surprise, then, for the job in DC would indeed become a nightmare.

Chapter 9

In 1995, a group of IBEW International Reps decided they were going to organize—become a union within a union. One might assume the IBEW would wholeheartedly favor the move; instead, management crushed it with an antilabor campaign more fervent than any "evil" corporation out there. It was the irony of the century, and some would say, one of the many signs of labor's impending demise. If the union heads were so confident in what they were selling, why wouldn't they have supported the efforts of their own employees to organize? I also should have heeded it as a sign that I should get the heck out of dodge. But when I heard about it at the 1996 IBEW convention—the same one at which Mike Lucas ran his valiant yet unsuccessful campaign against Jack Barry—I did not dwell on it. Union drama had nothing to do with me.

I had overt warnings as well. When upon hearing I was moving to the international someone quipped, "So they performed the lobotomy?" I was only slightly less confused when another person asked me, point blank, on my first day in DC: "What are you doing here, Brian?"

To me, the answer was a no-brainer: I was here to build upon my other work. For years I'd worked within the IBEW to effect positive change for workers, first at Local 1260 and then as an International rep. Now, as director of industrial organizing, I had the opportunity to effect wide-sweeping changes to the union's organizing strategies across the U.S. and Canada. In short, I still believed I was serving a purpose.

On a personal note, the move to Washington, DC, should have been the moment that let me know I had "arrived," no matter that my ten-thousand-dollar raise was eaten up by the higher taxes in the national's capital; it was all in service to a higher purpose. Just as it is the political epicenter of this country, Washington was the hub of the labor movement; it was like Rome to the Roman Empire. For someone who had come up in a small local, especially one as isolated as Hawaii, to the huge glass-and-steel office building on the corner of 7th Street NW, it was an enormous coup.

That was the perception, anyway. The reality was that working for the International was a quagmire of mind-numbing bureaucracy and red tape. The president, Ed Hill, controlled everything from the big-ticket policy items to the smallest minutia. Nothing escaped his notice, and his reactions to various people and situations were often contradictory, arbitrary, and known only to him. The office, I would learn, was populated mostly with his friends and political allies. It took me awhile to figure out why he had asked me to work there: between my organizing wins and my lack of previous ties to him, I brought credibility to Hill's tenure as president.

That said, no one on his staff, regardless of their rank or experience, was allowed to keep envelopes in their office, because God forbid a letter or memo went out without his signature. Each day, as the lunch hour drew to a close, he could be found lurking at the doors, waiting to catch anyone who was a minute late. Anyone who did incurred his wrath and possibly some sort of punishment. The Cold War had been over for years, but I felt like I was behind the Iron Curtain.

I was expected to be at my desk each morning by eight thirty, and but for sixty precious minutes for lunch, remain shackled there until four thirty. It was basically shift work in a suit and tie, which everyone was required to wear, despite the fact that we rarely saw anyone other than each other. I came to see that suit and tie as representative of the whole experience—a thin façade of professionalism hiding a culture of autocracy and mediocrity.

Visitors were far and few between, which was fine because of the ridiculous amount of bureaucracy one had to wade through in order to get "approval." Not even spouses were exempt. One day, Marilyn called to tell me she was in the area and wanted to pop in.

"I'll meet you in the lobby," I replied. Just the thought of engaging the arduous visitor "vetting" process was exhausting. Plus, for all I knew, the office was bugged and some IT person a few doors down would listen to our whole conversation and report it back to Hill.

An undercurrent of tension ran through every conversation, even in the air itself. It did not matter what position one held; everyone—even those in Hill's good graces—cracked their office doors and peeped out to see if anyone was coming down the hallway before emerging. I don't think they even knew what they were afraid of; we just had this general feeling that the rug could be ripped out from under us at any moment. Back in Hawaii—and to a large extent Nevada—all we thought about was the average worker, whether he was a current union member or a prospective one. In DC, everyone was worried far too much about their own butts to think of anyone else. Everyone knew the deal; when asked how they were doing, the stock answer was, "Living the dream," followed by a snicker. It wasn't long before I realized that no one ever wanted to go to DC.

Even in our offices we had no privacy. Many employers surveil their staff's Internet activity, but the IBEW took it to a new level. Every computer had tracking devices, and I commonly saw the cursor move when I looked at my screen, controlled remotely by the long arm of Big Brother as it checked my documents and browsing history. The first time I saw it, I thought I was imagining things. It was easier to think I was going crazy than to believe I had gone from complete professional autonomy to this gilded cage where my every movement, word, and thought was monitored. It was a system designed to extinguish any and all creative thought and impulse to act independently.

• • •

The IBEW had several departments, including industrial, telecommunications, broadcasting, utilities, and manufacturing. Shortly after I got to DC, Hill asked me to put together videos showcasing each department to put on the website. He seemed pleased when I told him I would develop the strategy, then run it by him.

Excited about having a role in crafting the IBEW's message, I reached out to the department directors. After explaining the project, I asked each director if he/she would prepare a two-minute script for the video. They were happy to comply, and when I had all the scripts ready, I scheduled the shooting. All was going according to plan, until I told Hill.

"What?" he screamed. "You're not supposed to do anything unless you have my permission!"

I stared back at him, shocked at his tone and completely nonplussed as to the reason for his anger. "But Ed, I didn't do anything yet. All I did was get everything ready—you still have to sign off on everything." When he didn't answer me, I decided to call his bluff. "I'll go the media center and tell them to forget it."

He paused for a second, perhaps thinking how it might look if he suddenly cancelled the project.

"No, you go ahead," he said finally, "but make sure I see every-thing, step by step."

I was a man in my forties with grown children and decades of experience, yet as I walked out of his office, I felt like a chastised toddler.

They wanted ideas, I realized, but didn't really want me to put them in motion. It never seemed to be the "right time," and while I never knew exactly what they meant, I knew it had nothing to do with benefitting the members, and everything to do with political expediency. When I did act and achieved success, they got nervous.

One would think that in such a controlled environment any sort of lascivious behavior would be severely punished. Instead, it was often swept under the rug, so long as the transgressor was in Hill's good graces. Each month, our esteemed president met with the directors, usually over a meal. These meetings were for the most part overwhelmingly dull, for he typically liked to discuss the same topics over and over again. There were always exceptions, however; for example, the day he decided to admonish us—*again*—against taking long lunches. Now, as we sat around, each wondering what shoe was about to drop next, he announced that it was okay if we had alcoholic beverages during the lunch hour, so long as we had no more than four. Four drinks . . . inside of an hour? Such an amount to be acceptable to a boss was unfathomable to me. Even I, who was no lightweight, would be drunk if I pounded four drinks in such a short time. Before long, though, I understood that some people needed the booze to get through the day.

The director of manufacturing, a nice man, had to be carried out of the building once or twice a week, completely ripped. And he wasn't the only one seen staggering out of various Seventh Street eateries. How else could one get through their days, knowing they had no purpose, feeling like they were simply rotting away?

On Christmas Day I was unwrapping gifts with my grandchildren when my cell phone beeped with a voice mail. When I listened to it and heard the familiar voice of one of the other directors at the IBEW, my mouth hung open in shock. "Brian, I need your help . . . I am in jail."

Apparently he had been at a gas station when he was approached by a young woman. They spoke for a few moments during which he had agreed to pay her for sex. That's when she whipped out her badge and informed him she was a cop. My colleague was calling me from the pokey, hoping that I would leave my family on Christmas to come bail him out. When I didn't answer the phone, he was forced to call his wife. She initiated divorce proceedings shortly after. The IBEW was much more forgiving. In fact, other than two weeks of rehab, followed by AA meetings—for which he left the office at one o'clock—he faced no professional consequences. Of course, this may have been due to the fact that he was the grandson of a previous IBEW president.

"Why would he do that?" Ed Hill asked incredulously when he found out. "There are so many girls in the building—he can screw them!"

Hill spoke from experience. While he was coming up at a local in Pennsylvania, several "incidents" involving Hill and female employees had to be settled out of court. Apparently the IBEW hadn't seen this as a liability, because he had still risen through the ranks. By the time I got there, he'd been carrying on a years-long extramarital affair with one of the directors, who was also married. Everyone knew of the affair—and that it was the reason she had her position. In his role as president, Ed travelled quite a bit to different locals and union strongholds throughout the country. On one of these trips he'd met this woman, found her attractive, and in true union style decided not only to hire her, but place her in a high-ranking position, responsible for literally tens of thousands of workers. This would not have been so bad if she were qualified, but she held a relatively low-level position and had absolutely no idea how to manage a department of that magnitude and importance. In the years that followed, her inexperience would be glaringly obvious; one only had to look at the union's rapidly shrinking slice of the pie in that area.

Chapter 10

In 2005, five unions representing 5.5 million workers broke from the AFL-CIO and formed an alternative umbrella organization called "Change to Win." These groups, including the International Brotherhood of Teamsters, the Service Employees International, and the United Farm Workers were concerned with the lack of effective organizing efforts on the part of the AFL-CIO and believed, quite rightly, that if labor continued on this course it would eventually fade into obscurity. Change to Win would focus the bulk of its financial and human resources on bringing new members in. This, of course, presented a real PR problem for labor. After all, unions were supposed to be all about presenting a united front; it was their strength at the bargaining table. But what about when those unions were weighted down by inertia and illusions of their own grandeur? The rogue unions contended that their members had, in effect, been disenfranchised. There was talk a few years later about the Change to Win returning to the AFL-CIO fold. The fact they didn't indicated a persistent conflict about the future of labor and who should lead it.

As the director of industrial organizing, my objective was clear: increase membership throughout the IBEW—meaning the U.S. and Canada. In my opinion, the best way to accomplish this was to implement strategic organizing. It was the same method I had employed in Guam four years earlier, albeit with more time and a lot more money. There were already people in the field all over the country. I wanted to step up these efforts by sending "swat teams" into a given area and mobilizing them. The first step to preparing a campaign was the research, from the targeted geographical area to the specific industry and, in corporate campaigns, the particular company. Next, we would prepare the area by going to job fairs, setting up booths at professional expos, and making TV commercials. After six months of this, we would finally send in the organizers. This method was essentially what I had done in Guam, but with more staff and more funding . . . or so I thought. The International certainly had the money to donate to the campaign—in fact, they had raised the per capita dues one dollar a year for five years, specifically for organizing efforts. Yet when it came time to spend that money on efforts to save the union in the coming years, they kept it clamped tightly in their meaty little fists.

Hill was misery even when it came to his pet organizing project. He wanted me to "rebuild the South," specifically Florida and North Carolina—a mission that in my opinion, and according to available data, made no sense. There was no "rebuilding" the South, it was more like building it from scratch. It was historically less friendly to labor than other regions; in fact, the southern states had the lowest union density. Moreover, both Florida and North Carolina were right-to-work states, which would make it exponentially harder to organize there. If we hoped to have any success at all, we would need not only boots on the ground, but door hangers, booths at craft fairs, and television commercials. Of course, this would cost a lot of money, which Hill did not want to invest. Instead, he preferred to saddle me with the friends he hired as payment for one favor or another but often had no idea what they were doing. It was as if he wanted the effort to fail. Then he could blame it on evil corporations and right-wing politics, trying to keep the workers down, when in reality all he wanted to do was keep me in my place.

His attitude was indicative of how out of touch the International was. The people there had no idea how to use social media, nor could they communicate messages. They didn't understand that the modern worker was generally more educated and more aware of his/ her own needs; they also wanted to move up the ranks based on their own merit, rather than seniority. Even worse, they were unwilling to learn from others; to them it meant they were losing control of their rapidly shrinking turf.

I saw things differently. Back in 1995, I had travelled Japan as an ambassador of the IBEW. I toured a plant at Fukishima and studied their labor market as well as their union equivalent. I noted a mutual respect between the company and the workers; the workers felt they were treated well and in turn were loyal to the company. It was a relationship based on mutual respect. Interestingly, the unions were considered part of the company, which in my opinion was a smart move.

I tried to turn lemons to lemonade, which is to say I tried to imbue my forty-person department—the largest in the IBEW—with a sense of purpose while sidestepping Hill's minefield of protocols, policies, and unwritten rules that he seemed to make up as he went along. I created a reporting system for those under me—including the ten international reps and clerical staff in the office, as well as seven regional coordinators who managed the organizers in the field. I held regular staff meetings so everyone could check in and feel part of a cohesive team. Slowly but surely, I began building a model for organizing success. It was a strategic model based on researching a given area for receptivity to the union, followed by the training and education of the workers there. At the beginning of a campaign I would send out an email blast to encourage the team and set the goal in numbers of new members we wanted to sign. Each time, I set the number higher, and each time my team met the goal. Before long we had a 75 percent "win" rate.

While at Local 1260, I didn't remember ever feeling boxed in by the International. We were free to advocate for workers as we saw fit, including negotiating deals that also benefitted the company rather than treating them like the Big Bad Wolf. Now, as I saw how controlling the folks in Washington, DC, were, I had to wonder whether perhaps they'd simply seen Hawaii as small potatoes. Whatever the case, I was grateful Local 1260 had flown under the radar; I also drew from the experience to create an organizing model that sought to strike a balance between the International and local autonomy. Unfortunately, my ideas often met with a great deal of resistance from the others on the International staff. When I arrived, the International had no organizing model to speak of, yet when I told my colleagues that what they were doing was not working, they cut me off.

"You don't understand, Brian," they'd say so often, it became like a mantra.

Within the first year of my arrival, membership had increased from 685,000 members to 725,000. Elated and energized, I figured this was surely enough to silence the naysayers. I was wrong. Instead of being pleased with our success, Hill tried to put the brakes on it.

"Don't get ahead of yourself with the numbers, Brian," he'd say, trying to adopt a light-hearted, almost fatherly tone, as if trying to spare me the disappointment of falling short of my goals. The only thing he cared about was protecting his own turf.

While I had no designs on his office, I did, in pursuing my goals, threaten to expose the incompetency at the International. Vice presidents from around the country would call and ask me to speak at their annual conferences. As with everything else, I had to get Hill's approval in order to go. At first, he basically rubber-stamped these requests, but as more and more requests for me came in, he started to feel threatened, and his approvals decreased accordingly.

At a meeting in Connecticut, I asked what was going on with freelance photo journalists—a group of people I thought we might target, given their growing prominence with the field.

Ed Hill was there, as was his paramour. They tried to play it off, but from the looks on their faces they clearly had no idea what a freelance photo journalist was! I shouldn't have been surprised—Hill didn't even know what a corporate campaign was, and that had been an organizing staple since the 1970s. Labor would choose a target company, either because they had a problem with it specifically or because it stood in the way of the achievement of some social justice goal, then run a relentless attack on it. The goal was to undermine the target so badly—with board members, customers, et cetera—that it was forced to make concessions to the union. Another word comes to mind for the corporate campaign: blackmail.

Chapter 11

In her 2005 book, *Finding Our Way: Leadership for an Uncertain Time*, organizational consultant Margaret J. Wheatley wrote, "For me, this is a familiar image—people in the organization ready and willing to do good work, wanting to contribute their ideas, ready to take responsibility, and leaders holding them back, insisting that they wait for decisions or instructions." Though Wheatley was writing about organizations in general, it seemed especially apropos of my experience at the International, and of the malaise afflicting labor in general.

By the time my one-year anniversary rolled around, I was ready to wash my hands of the whole thing. On the surface, I had a career anyone would dream of—a fancy title at a swanky location; I earned a good living and had a comfortable home. I even got a few perks, including an invite to the Emmy Awards. But whether I was sitting at my desk or walking the red carpet with Marilyn by my side, I was painfully aware that it was all window dressing. After decades of meaningful work, I had reached the pinnacle of the IBEW, only to find it came at a steep price: I was expected to be a drone. Having to seek Ed Hill's approval before completing the smallest task was bad enough; what made it intolerable was that he could never give me an answer as to what he wanted. He would simply offer vague parameters, then use my best efforts as an example of what he was *not* looking for. It was maddening. In 2007, I went to Hill's office and asked for a few minutes of his time. He waved me toward a seat in front of his desk.

"I can't work in this environment," I said without preamble. "I can't get anything done here."

As I laid out all the frustration I'd been feeling, Hill stared at me with a confused, almost vacant look in his eye. I felt like I was speaking a language he did not understand, which in a way was the truth. How many years had it been since he was connected to any sense of a mission?

Finally, I said, "I want to go back to the Ninth District."

Hill's confusion deepened to shock. I appreciated seeing at least a change in his expression; otherwise I couldn't be sure he'd heard a word I said.

"But Brian," he said after a moment, "no one leaves DC."

I glanced around, half-expecting to hear "Hotel California" being piped into the room.

After perhaps the most frustrating and one-sided conversation of my life, I slipped out of his office. Although I didn't yell or scream, inside I was seething. It was not yet quitting time, but I couldn't have cared less as I grabbed my car keys and walked out of the building. I felt like I was making some great escape.

"We're getting out of here," I said to a shocked Marilyn when I arrived home.

After tossing a few things in a bag, we were back in the car, heading west. Two days and two stops in Indiana and Colorado, we at last arrived in Vegas with our family. By that time, Marilyn and I had become grandparents three times over: Brandon and Neiani had a son, Payton, and a daughter, Paige, and Megan and Eric had a son, Kaeden. I didn't necessarily intend to quit my job—I just knew I needed to get out of that dreadful place for a while. I needed freedom. Most of all, I needed to feel like myself again, and spending time with my children and grandchildren was the best medicine.

If my words didn't let Hill know I meant business, my flight from DC did. When he called my cell a few days later, he was full of aw shucks, apologies, and promises—the same jovial charmer who had offered me the job. Things would be better, he said, if I came back; the International would open itself up to new concepts. It wasn't that the IBEW didn't want to change with the times; sometimes it just took time and the right person to implement it. That person, according to Hill, was me.

I bought it hook, line, and sinker. Not the part about Hill believing that I was *the* right person—I knew when I was being schmoozed— but about the ability of the International to evolve and grow. By the end of the week I had shipped the car back East. As Marilyn and I boarded our plane, I tried to convince myself that positive changes were in store.

I was wrong, of course. Nothing changed. In fact, if anything, things got worse. The director of broadcasting was caught communicating with women on a sex chat room scandal using his office computer during work hours. He was terminated by the IBEW, not because they were worried about the morality (or lack thereof) of his behavior, but because they were worried the Department of Labor would find out. The department had recently audited the IBEW, including Hill's regular trips on a private plane, and he was terrified of further scrutiny. As for the director of broadcasting, he was friends with several union higher-ups and was therefore allowed to resign. The International even helped him get a job with Frontier Communications, a company up north.

Others, like a man from the Construction Department, did something that earned him a reassignment to the "Research Department." This was essentially a no-man's-land for those whose transgressions did not merit a firing but were too severe to be completely swept under the rug. He would remain there for the next twenty years, all but forgotten by everyone else in the building. He did get a lot of research done; it just had nothing to do with the IBEW. Instead, he embarked on an intensive genealogy project. Each day he'd come in, unplug his laptop from the mainframe so it could not be monitored, and trace his roots. Then, promptly at four thirty, he would save his "work" on a thumb drive and go home. Not a bad gig, if your top career priorities are surviving the day and collecting a paycheck.

In a year full of frustration, one significant bright spot came when Brandon and Megan moved their families to Virginia to be closer to me and Marilyn. When someone at nearby Potomac Power told me the company had apprenticeship openings, I told them I knew two "kids" who would make excellent candidates. Brandon and Eric each had to go a lengthy process that included taking tests, then flying back East for interviews, but they were both hired as apprentices, with a goal of becoming substation technicians. We also welcomed another family member—Megan and Eric's daughter Meadow—into the world. With all of us reunited, I reminded myself how truly blessed I was, and that nothing that happened at the IBEW could ever change that.

• • •

"Unions would never again enjoy a political environment as favorable as that which transformed American work life between 1934 and 1937." These words from famed labor historian Nelson Lichten-stein perfectly described another huge hurdle I faced in DC: the decades-long downslope of the labor movement. Union density had decreased throughout the country, thanks in part to an increase in right-to-work states, and the IBEW was not immune. To me, the reason for the decrease was no mystery: those in charge of running labor—and the politicians they were in bed with—were betraying its most basic credo, the first and only priority to act on behalf of the American worker and, by extension, America itself.

Time was labor's greatest enemy. In the 1930s, a desperate public turned its favor toward labor, in part because of the Depression but also because it was supported by FDR. Like the president, unions were seen as champions for social justice on several fronts, including healthcare, workman's comp, and pensions. Mainly, unions were seen as fighting the arbitrary powers of employers. These days, laborers are much more educated, technologically savvy, and aware of their rights; moreover, 90 percent of what unions used to lobby for are now encapsulated in law. Those in union management positions, on the other hand, are not particularly educated or techy—they simply knew the right people and as a result had been promoted to positions they are ill-equipped to handle. Afraid of losing their cushy jobs, they refuse to think outside the box, instead preferring to bury their heads in the sand and pretend they are living during labor's heyday.

Millions around the world saw the election of Barack Obama in 2008 as a symbol of progress, hope, and sweeping social reforms. This sentiment was echoed throughout the Labor Movement, with leaders and members alike touting his victory as a step for the working man and congratulating themselves for the role they played in it.

The new president hit the ground running with an ambitious domestic agenda, starting with making healthcare affordable to everyone. However, a lesser-known measure that had specifically to do with unions also topped his list. It was called the Employee Free Choice Act, but like many laws, its true meaning ran counter to its name.

The act had three main tenets, the most important of which was the "card check" provision. Every union has representation cards that, during a campaign, potential members could sign and give to the organizer ahead of the election. The Employee Free Choice Act would allow unions to use these cards as a means of circumventing elections. If the organizer was able to present the National Labor Relations Board with signed cards for 50 percent plus one of the workers, the company would automatically become a union shop. The second provision imposed binding arbitration on companies who opposed signing the union contract, while the third increased the monetary penalties for firing organizers and engaging in other so-called "union avoidance" activities.

Pro-labor organizations such as the Center for American Progress Action Fund lobbied hard on behalf of the bill. They claimed that the right to unionize was under attack by right-wing politicians and that the election process had been corrupted by employers who used threats and intimidation to keep workers in line. The card check provision, they contended, would go a long way to "balancing" the process and even reverse the decline of unions in the country.

Although I supported Obama and even attended his inauguration on that bitterly cold January day, I could not in good conscious get behind this bill. First, I felt that all three provisions unfairly bound companies. Any Joe Schmoe could sign those cards—no verification process ensured they were legitimate "votes." Second, the bill robbed workers of their voice. Organizers had little incentive to educate workers as to why joining the union was beneficial or what they would be getting for their dues. For this reason, it flew in the face of everything labor claimed it stood for.

To me, the point of organizing was to engage and educate the hearts and minds of workers and allow them to determine for themselves whether they needed a third party to negotiate on their behalf. Sneaking in the back door, which was essentially what the act would allow labor to do, was lazy; it also robbed both the companies and workers of the opportunity to create relationships based on trust rather than strong-arming. Finally, the authors and proponents of the bill blamed everyone under the sun for labor's decline . . . everyone except labor. The bill simply reaffirmed what I had seen in DC for the past two years—leaders were completely out of touch with both workers and companies. Moreover, it showed their refusal to accept responsibility for their own ineptitude.

I was not alone in this standpoint. No one was surprised that employers were vehemently opposed to the idea; however, it was a bit of a shock that both the House and Senate shot down the bill, despite both being controlled by the Democrats. Not even after the union softened their position and said members could either sign the card *or* vote could Obama convince his compatriots to vote for it.

Chapter 12

The inability to pass the Employee Free Choice Act was a significant disappointment for labor leaders. They had come out in full force for Obama during the election season, particularly around the issue of healthcare reform, only to have a measure they supported die on the vine and get pushed to the wayside. If unions wanted to attract new members, they were going to have to get out there and work for them. It was a tough pill to swallow, and it wouldn't be the only one.

When the Great Recession hit in 2008, many thought unions would once again rise to prominence. Instead, the opposite was true. When the economy was good, labor's lackadaisical attitude was sufficient to manage the slow but steady decline in membership, revenue, and influence at the bargaining table. Bad times, however, accelerated union losses and made labor part of the national conversation on politics and the economy. Unlike the Depression, the Great Recession would serve only to further weaken labor. In the 1930s, unions were seen as champions, a bulwark standing between working families and breadlines; now they were considered to have a stranglehold on the economy, mostly in the form of bloated yet underfunded pension plans that threatened to bankrupt state governments. In the private sector, companies fearful of the future and protective of their dwindling profit margins were able to hire nonunion, temporary workers who made a smaller hourly wage and did not have benefits. They didn't care that union members made more money and had the Cadillac of health insurance plans; they felt fortunate to be working and able to put food on the table. This weakened unions' power, both at the bargaining table and on the picket line. When union members went out on strike, plenty of "scabs" usually waited to take their place. At the IBEW, membership dropped back down to 685,000.

While I understood the enormous and wide-reaching ramifications of the recession, I still believed we could increase membership or at least stem the bleeding with some strategic corporate campaigns and outside-the-box thinking. Leadership, however, threw up their hands and decided to ride it out. Their messaging at that time began and ended with, "See, banks are the bad guys."

One day, during the height of the recession, I received a call from a woman who declined to give her name. She didn't know who I was either—she had just called the International's number and happened to get transferred to my extension. I recognized something familiar in her voice, though, and as she began to tell me the reason for her call, I realized what it was: desperation. It was like when I turned on the news and learned of another depressing unemployment figure or saw another family whose home had been foreclosed upon.

At first when she told me her husband was an out-of-work union member, I thought she was asking me to get him a job. Turned out it was a little more complicated than that. Unlike so many other people, it had been easy for him to find work—the problem was it was all nonunion.

I knew what was coming next, even before she said it. The local warned him not to take the work; if he did, they would ruin him professionally. And they could do it, too—unions often employed "salts," or people that got jobs in nonunion places to spy on workers. If there happened to be salts where he took a job, they would report back to the local. In the meantime, the couple was worried about making their mortgage payments. Talk about being between the proverbial rock and hard place. Labor was supposed to be protecting workers, and instead they were strong-arming them like some gang of thugs. I thought about her dilemma for a minute, knowing there was really only one thing I could say.

"You need to do what you need to do to feed your family."

It was risky to take nonunion work, I told her, but not as risky as having no paycheck at all. I didn't mention, however, the risk *I* was taking in giving her such counsel. If word ever got out, I would have been out on the street, and forget about ever getting my pension. All I could do was pray that my phones weren't tapped.

To my knowledge, no one ever found out what I said to her; she, on the other hand, called me back a few months later to say thank you. Apparently her husband had followed my advice and taken whatever work was available to him, even though it was nonunion. They had been able to keep their home and, while things were not perfect, the family was hanging in there. Before we hung up, she thanked me again, but I found myself feeling grateful to her. I so rarely had the chance to interact with the people my work was supposedly helping.

A major part of my job consisted of workarounds—an effort to circumvent, not the big bad employers trying to prevent workers from unionizing, but the iron-fisted bureaucracy of my so-called "brothers" at the union. Each day my greatest challenge was to navigate the myriad rules and regulations and carve out a pathway to success. And we did experience many successes, including a 75 percent win rate, meaning my organizers in the field won three out of four elections. While these were certainly meaningful, I felt as though they were merely chipping at an enormous boulder. They did not achieve my larger goal, namely, to drag labor into this century and change the way they approached the business of empowering the American worker.

Still, I learned to take my victories where I could get them. More importantly, I learned from those we did not win, and sought to incorporate those learnings into the IBEW's organizing model. One of the most critical was the effort to organize National Cash Register (NCR). It was, for a number of reasons, one of the more challenging campaigns I'd ever run, but it would also turn out to be one of the most valuable.

NCR was a true American success story. Started in Ohio in 1884, it designed and sold the first motorized cash register. Since then it had made everything from weaponry in World Wars I and II to various types of computers. It was acquired by AT&T and then broke free again, and it had grown into an international conglomerate, but it was still primarily known for cash registers and ATMs to stores in every corner of the globe. I now had them in my sights. The company fell under one of the jurisdictions we most wanted to beef up—telecommunications. In addition, my organizers in the field had done some research and found them to be a viable target.

When I announced my intention to run an integrated national campaign, I knew I would experience blowback. Not for any particular reason, mind you, but because I encountered blowback when I tried to do anything at the International. First, it was from the attorneys on retainer for IBEW, offering their services. "I got this covered," I told them. Well, this didn't go over too well. Like everyone else in DC, they were used to a certain way of doing things and used to everyone having a place; they didn't like the idea of someone stepping out of it.

"There is legal stuff around petitioning and other aspects of the campaign that you will need to have a good understanding of."

"But I do understand these things," I said carefully. I wanted to tell them that I had more than a decade of experience in contract negotiations under my belt long before coming to DC. I also wanted to point out that their services were overused, at the expense of the members. But, since being diplomatic had become part and parcel of my job, from the smallest minutiae to issues of the greatest importance, I held my tongue. "If I need your help," I told them, "I will certainly ask for it." They acted cordial enough, but I could tell from their expressions that they thought I would soon be coming to them. I determined right then and there that I would not, and instead started outlining my campaign strategy.

Although NCR had offices everywhere, I specifically targeted workers in Southern California and Arizona. As I would soon find out, a significant hurdle to my plan also presented a unique opportunity. Per rules set up under President George W. Bush, the National Labor Relations Board had designated organizing "regions" throughout the country, with regard to certain companies. This meant any attempts to organize the employees of these companies would have to be done in blocks, and therefore exponentially more difficult. There could only be one election per block, so if for example, a union wanted to organize workers in Missouri, and that state was part of a block that included Illinois and Ohio, they would have to campaign—and win over enough employees—in all three states. As those at the International were quick to tell me, this included NCR. This had been determined at a hearing, they said, long before I came along, and although I never knew the specific rationale behind the decision, I strongly suspected it was all about crippling the organizing efforts. Arizona and California were in the same block, yet something told me I should test the water and attempt to have them petition the NLRB separately.

In the meantime, I instructed my organizers in the field—several in Southern California and one in Arizona—to meet with NCR employees and get a read on how receptive they were to unionizing. They soon got back to me with the good news: we had major interest in both states.

When I told them I wanted to petition California separately, Ed Hill and his cohorts thought I was crazy. "It is not going to work, Brian. This is an established rule." Well, I had worked with government agencies long enough to know that rules and regulations often outlived their usefulness. Sometimes people forgot they were even on the books.

I made concessions on a daily basis; this time I stood my ground. "What's the worst they can do? Come back and say we have to petition in Arizona too?" I pointed out that we had enough interest in Arizona and should be able to win an election outright in that state as well. I just wanted to give this a try.

"Guess you know what you're doing," Hill said. He looked around the room at his cronies, who nodded their agreement. "We would do it differently . . ."

I shrugged. "Well, I guess you'll have to trust me on this one."

"We don't necessarily trust you," Hill said, and the others chuckled, "but we'll let you do what you have to do."

Sure enough, the NLRB accepted the California petition, with no mention of Arizona. Encouraged by the news, I instructed my organizers to continue the campaign process, the most important aspect of which was to keep NCR's employees engaged. I wanted more than anything to be there with them, talking to the workers, hearing about their needs and explaining to them the benefits of having the support and representation of the IBEW. This direct interaction was where I had always hit my stride and reconnected to the meaning of the work. This time, however, it was not to be. Ed Hill would never approve my leaving the office. Instead, I had to run everything over conference calls and emails with the regional coordinator, who then hopefully energized the team.

"Let's do this," I said, "and let's do it right." At the time, another NLRB rule designated a six-week window between petition and union election. This was also burdensome, for it meant organizers had to maintain a high level of excitement among the workers, lest they lose interest. Eventually, President Obama would, by executive order, shorten that window to two weeks, but in the meantime we had to work with what we had, and I decided to use the extra time to my advantage.

When she heard about the activity in California, my organizer in Arizona was chomping at the bit to put her petition in as well.

"We're going to do that," I told her, "but let's wait a little bit."

In the meantime, I had something else planned.

When I told the team we were going to use secondary pressure, they acted like I had three heads. I couldn't believe that supposedly seasoned union guys didn't know about this important component of a corporate campaign.

First, I was going to go to the IBEW's research department and ask them to get me a list of NCR's biggest customers. Then I would choose one that interacted directly with the public; we would then put enough pressure on that company to hopefully cause them financial "discomfort." The goal was for them to turn around and say to NCR, "What are you guys doing? Why don't you just work with the union?" Perhaps they may even threaten to end their business relationship.

I scanned the list of NCR's customers and immediately decided that Victoria's Secret would give us the most bang for our buck. The stores were usually in malls or other crowded shopping areas that had plenty of foot traffic and would easily garner attention. I then chose twelve areas around the country—Minnesota, Seattle, New York, Oregon, and Northern California among them—where we would gain the most impact (for example, the Mall of America just outside Minneapolis) and steered clear of Arizona and Southern California so as not to interfere with our organizing efforts. After another conference call to the organizers in those areas, we were good to go.

On the designated date and time, the organizers and a small army of volunteers showed up to those Victoria Secret locations and, for the next two hours, passed out hand bills. We had no problem getting men to hand them out; they lined up when they heard we were targeting Victoria Secrets. The specific message was carefully crafted so the IBEW would not get into any legal trouble, stating NCR was an unfair company that was infringing upon its employees' right to seek union representation. It went off without a hitch. Women considering shopping there were turned off by the crowd of men, and sales suffered during that time. A lot of the volunteers got booted by mall security, but even this added to the drama and the impact.

Ed Hill could not understand what I was trying to accomplish. "Why are you going to places that have nothing to do with NCR?" he asked. "Why wouldn't you hand bill in areas where you are trying to organize?"

I swallowed my own question: *How does someone become president of an entire union without knowing how to run a corporate campaign?* The event was not about causing significant damage to Victoria's Secret or even to NCR, but about showing NCR that we could, in fact, affect their customers, and by extension, them. Hence the term secondary pressure.

Instead, I simply said, "Because we don't need to." By that time the election was about three weeks out. We had already stipulated—or "stipped"—with the company, meaning that both NCR and the IBEW agreed that there was nothing to stop the election from moving forward and were waiving their right to a pre-election hearing with the NLRB. The company had also filed the Excelsior list, or the names of employees eligible to vote. That's when I gave the Arizona organizer the green light to file her petition.

Once again, the NLRB accepted the petition, with no mention of the regional blocks. I had succeeded in qualifying a law that had severely tied labor's hands for years. It was an enormous win.

By that time the campaign in Arizona was rapidly losing steam. This was a common enough problem in organizing campaigns, and for myriad reasons—perhaps the management team there had started listening to the workers or the employees just decided unionizing was too much trouble. Most likely, the reason was because we only had one organizer down there. My goal at that point was to use Arizona to leverage the election in California by diverting NCR's funds and focus. Now they would have to put out a fire in Arizona as well, and this would require moving resources there. It would also gain media attention, which in turn would further galvanize employees in California.

With its twists and turns, the campaign was an organizer's dream. As the election drew near, the organizers in California assured me that we would win. But, like any election, it's not over until it's over, and at the end of the day the employees chose not to join the union. Like any loss, it stung a bit, and I'm not sure whether the fact that we lost by only ten points or so made it better or worse. What bothered me most was the faulty intel I had gotten from the boots on the ground, most of whom had been chosen by Ed Hill. Would things have been different if I had been able to be there? I would never know, and that made it all the more frustrating.

At the end of the day, though, this was a victory. I had taught the International a different way to organize, namely, how to use different leverage points. At the time, this method was not being used at all; organizers were still going into companies to "hammer it home" about how employees were better off if they joined the union. The NCR campaign, although ultimately unsuccessful, provided a model of how to run a corporate campaign. It began with researching the target company, then strategizing based on that information. We could run a top-down campaign whereby we talked to the employer about benefits of having a union shop, or we could run a regular NLRB campaign.

I had also proved that we did not have to just blindly follow the NLRB. If we wanted to significantly increase—and retain—membership, we had to start thinking and acting outside the box. If Ed Hill appreciated this rationale, he gave no indication. He simply marked it in the "loss" column.

I scheduled another conference call with my team to analyze the campaign. It was something I did after every election, win or lose. It was one more thing my colleagues thought was odd. For them, a win meant slapping each other on the back and making the assumption that everything had been done right. To me, this was lazy and counterproductive. There was always room for improvement.

I hadn't invented this; I'd learned it from football. Ask any coach in the NFL, and he'll tell you that after winning a game, after the cheering and drinking and partying, the next day is spent going over films to see what they'd done right and what mistakes they had made. It helped them enhance good decisions and fix the problems. It was the best way to improve for the next time.

My version of Monday quarterbacking was similar. I'd go down a list of ten components of organizing to evaluate every aspect of the campaign, including secondary pressure, political pressure, house calling, cold calling, and meetings with employees. I'd also ask basic but important questions such as, did we have at least one organizer for every hundred employees? Did we check the demographics of the groups we were trying to organize? Did we have an organizer of color? Again, this was not my invention, but based on a Cornell University study. It listed these components and analyzed how employing them increases the possibility of winning. If you use three of the components, your chances are 30%; if you use seven, chances go up to 70%, and so on.

While the organizers on the ground understood, those at the International thought it was a wasted exercise; they just wanted to move on to the next campaign.

"Why do we need that?" became a commonly asked question.

I'd sigh and realize that once again my efforts had fallen on deaf ears.

Chapter 13

I experienced other significant achievements as well, but as time went on I felt more stifled, powerless, and worst of all, confused. My whole life I had believed that God had a plan and a purpose for everyone. For me, that purpose was helping to build a bridge between employers and workers so that both came to the bargaining table feeling valued and respected, and that in facilitating these relationships I was ultimately helping to strengthen America's middle class. After years of doing this at the local level, influencing national policy seemed the next logical step; however, I soon found that I missed that day-to-day contact with the workers and their employers. Moreover, I realized that much like the federal government itself, labor leaders had forgotten their purpose. What had started out as a movement to empower workers and effect social change was now just a large, bloated organism seeking only to protect its own butt.

As time wore on I noticed a marked change in my mood. I didn't have the same mental and physical energy that I used to, and I had a more difficult time being motivated. One day blended into the next, and no matter what I did or what strides I made, I would continue to ram smack into an insurmountable wall of bureaucracy, insecurity, and stubbornness. I needed a new perspective.

I had always been an introspective person, and saw great benefit in examining even deeply personal circumstances objectively. When I applied this to my current situation, it gave me pause. Thanks to my parents and teachers, both secular and religious, I had been given a foundation built on one core belief: regardless of the title we hold, where we live, and our level of education, we all inherently have value and a God-given purpose. The key to realizing this purpose was passion. We had to believe in something so bad that it hurt inside—not just work, but home and all aspects of life—and live it every day.

Up to that point, that belief had been reflected back to me by my experiences, whether I was raising my children or serving as shop steward back in Hawaii. I, in turn, had passed this along to my own children. I then thought of my current environment, which was the antithesis of this. The DC environment had slowly been seeping into my mind like contaminated water, and it was poisoning me. This was in part due to a pervasive lack of spirituality in labor, especially at the International. Their creed was not "power of the people" but "power of the people on top." What then of all the people who felt this way all the time, simply because they had not been given the same support I had? The waste of potential was staggering. On the heels of this realization was that the model labor operated under was even more antiquated than I had thought. Even in its best moments, labor was not helping workers find that purpose, but simply perpetuating a perceived antagonism with their employers.

It had taken me a while, but I finally realized I would not be able to effect such systemic change while under Ed Hill's thumb. I knew

I couldn't stay at the International for the rest of my working life, but where I would go from there, I had not the slightest clue. In the meantime, I got up each day in gratitude, reminding myself that I had my family, my health, and a lovely home. I made the most of my time off—dinners with Marilyn, strumming a guitar or singing karaoke, and playing a round of golf when I had the time. Sometimes Frank Sinatra and Tony Bennett were enough to lift my mood. And, in my lowest moments, I reminded myself that if you open yourself up to God, He will move you in a direction that will bring success.

I often wondered how my stint in DC would come to an end; none of my imagined scenarios, however, were even in the ballpark. One Saturday morning in 2010, I met Ed Hill and the secretary of the treasury at an IHOP in Falls Church, Virginia, to discuss a campaign in Baltimore that had not been going well. But what was supposed to be a breakfast-brainstorming session soon turned into an ambush.

We were in the middle of the discussion when Ed said, "Brian, I don't get it. When I was coming up, there was a nonunion electrical shop across the street from the local. And they are still nonunion today. Why is that, Brian?"

At first I thought the question was a philosophical one, but then I looked up at Ed and saw that he seemed agitated. I shrugged and told him I didn't know.

He leaned slightly forward in his chair. "What are you doing about it, Brian?"

So this was where he was going. "Ed, can I ask you a couple of questions?"

"Sure, but what are you going to do about it?"

"How long were you the business manager there?"

"Ten years."

"How come *you* never organized them?" My tone was respectful, but from the look on Ed's face I knew I had gotten my point across. I didn't care—I was not about to be bullied for not doing something he had never done himself.

This conversation was indicative of a larger struggle within labor. They were going through an identity process (they no longer knew who they were or what their place in the world was) but were unwilling to change. They just kept raising dues for ideas that would never be implemented. How many grand plans had I seen fade away over the years? I'd lost count. At one point they'd decided to make member identification cards, each with data such as where the person was working, whether or not his/her dues had been paid, and the length of membership. They spent millions designing the cards but never created them.

From there, the meeting quickly deteriorated. Hill accused me of screwing up the Baltimore campaign; then, suddenly, in the middle of the restaurant, he starting yelling that I had resigned from my position at the International. I left the IHOP thinking, *This is it. The old man has finally lost it.*

A few minutes later, my cell phone buzzed. I pulled it from my pocket and was surprised to see an email from Hill, sent to me and forty other people.

I regret to inform you that Brian Ahakuelo has announced his resignation . . .

What?

Ed answered on the first ring, like he'd been staring at the phone waiting for my call.

"What the hell is going on, Ed?"

As usual, he chose a rehearsed response in lieu of answering my question. "You'll stay on the payroll until I can figured out why you resigned."

"But I didn't resign, Ed."

"Oh yes you did."

On June 23, Ed and I met for a second meeting. I thought for sure he would ask me to let bygones be bygones, much as he had when I took off to Vegas three years earlier, but he just slid a piece of paper across the table.

"You can say you resigned."

If I heard the word resign one more time, I thought my head might explode. No way was I going to make this easy on him. When I refused to resign, Ed wasted no time in firing me. Now, this was a dance with which I was well acquainted. I got an attorney and threatened suit, and the IBEW made me a deal: I would keep my mouth shut, and they would pay me through the following December.

Once I was gone, they wasted no time getting a new director and staff; there had undoubtedly been a long line of drones waiting in the wings.

Chapter 14

On January 1, 1994, President Bill Clinton signed the North American Free Trade Agreement (NAFTA) into law, thereby sparking a twenty-plus-year battle for the hearts and minds of American workers and consumers alike.

"NAFTA means jobs," Clinton had stated back then. "American jobs, and good-paying American jobs. If I didn't believe that, I wouldn't support this agreement."

Indeed, he is alternately credited and blamed for the passage of the act, despite the fact that the American, Mexican, and Canadian governments had been negotiating it for a couple of years before he even took office. In addition, by the time the final bill reached Congress, it had garnered bipartisan support.

Ask any labor leader and he will tell you NAFTA has been a travesty. Unions claim that the agreement has redistributed wealth and power to corporations at the expense of the American workers, particularly those in California, Texas, Michigan, and other states with a lot of manufacturing jobs. NAFTA freed companies to move their factories and plants out of the country, which meant they also had the ability to threaten workers with relocation when it came to determining pay rates and even their right to unionize. As evidence, unions cite the 700,000 jobs that have flown south of the border; the stagnation of wages for jobs that did stay; and even the decline in union density across the country.

It appears, however, that NAFTA is a symptom of a larger problem, for since its passage companies have also outsourced jobs to China, India, and Japan. For all their chest-pounding about how NAFTA and other political moves have crippled the American worker and therefore the middle class, labor leaders have refused to acknowledge their own significant role. China, Japan, and Mexico did not come here to steal jobs. American companies left because it became too costly to do business here.

Once upon a time labor had indeed been the voice of the American worker. But somewhere along the line it became drunk on its own power. Case in point: in the days before NAFTA, the United Auto Workers had such a chokehold on the industry that they could demand almost whatever they wanted. Per their contract, a UAW worker could take a one-year leave and receive 95 percent of his pay! This wasn't some obscure, rarely used clause buried in the fine print, but a sweet perk utilized by thousands. These workers would actually look to get laid off, then ask their managers not to call them back to work until the gravy train ran out. The drain on the company's resources was astronomical; it drove up production costs, which in turn drove up costs to consumers. The UWA was hurting America, specifically the middle class it claimed to champion. To the union, the company was nothing more than a cash cow, and this attitude led not only to

NAFTA, but to union workers being priced right out of the labor market. Labor had clearly lost its way.

For someone like me, who had grown up in the days of George Meany, rules such as the UAW had were incredibly disheartening. What had once been a movement by and for the American worker—and by extension, America itself—had become a weapon used to hold our corporations hostage. Getting workers a fair, living wage was one thing; strong-arming companies into giving yearlong handouts did not instill in workers a sense of self-determination, it infantilized them and turned them into abusers of the system, rather than being a proactive part of it. At the same time, it also wounded companies who were the major employers. If they went out of business or moved away, where would that leave the American worker? This was a dangerous notion, I knew. As I had seen firsthand while working in the belly of beast, the IBEW was a political animal protecting its territory, and if you got in its way you were going to get crushed.

When things went sideways in DC, I felt as though I had been split in two. Part of me was deeply wounded by the way Ed Hill and his cronies had treated me. I felt like I had been duped—recruited by Hill because of my organizing chops, only to be put out to pasture. Another part of me was relieved, for I knew I could not have dealt with the totalitarian regime for the rest of my career. For six years I had done everything I could to fulfill my purpose, but none of it mattered. If I was being honest with myself, I'd been a thorn in Hill's side almost from the moment I'd gotten there.

The hell with them, I thought. Marilyn echoed that sentiment, for she had watched me come home from work each day a little less energetic than the day before. Slowly, the International was draining all sense of passion and purpose from me. When I announced that I was going to move on to something outside labor, I think she was more relieved than I was.

As we packed up our house and prepared to head out West, the only thing that saddened us was that we'd be leaving our family behind. Brandon and Eric were doing well at Potomac Energy, and Brandon served as shop steward for Local 1900. My daughter and daughter-in-law had also acclimated to life on the East Coast, and my grandchildren were happily ensconced in their schools. A move simply did not make sense for them; at least, not yet.

I soon found that moving on from labor was easier said than done. I put out feelers with various companies and soon was interviewing on a regular basis. I would leave each meeting on a high, thinking an offer was right around the corner, only to hear that they were "going in another direction" or had hired from within. At first I chalked it up to the lousy economy, but when one woman made me an offer, only to withdraw it a day later, a light bulb went off. As my former employer, the IBEW was getting calls about my qualifications, and clearly their responses had been less than glowing. They had blacklisted me. Labor regularly employed this tool in dealing with their enemies, but I had never seen it used under circumstances such as mine. I had done nothing to embarrass the IBEW; in fact, thanks to Ed Hill's email—and a confidential agreement I had signed with them—it appeared as though I had simply resigned my post.

After exhausting several avenues in California and Nevada, I heard that Starwood, an international chain of high-end resorts, was seeking a senior human resources manager at one of its Hawaii locations. So once again, Marilyn and I packed up our stuff and boarded a plane for home.

This time, I left nothing to chance. As soon as I walked out of the Starwood interview, I pulled out my cell and called the IBEW's office in DC. I knew what they had been doing, I told them, and it had better stop now. I got the job.

Although I had visited Hawaii whenever I could over the years, it was still a shock to the system when I returned to live there in 2011. Like most people, I'd unconsciously envisioned the place of my youth as unchanged, and like most people, I was wrong. The sugar cane fields of Pearl City had been replaced by mega chain stores like Walmart and Target. The cost of living, already astronomical in 1993 when "The Price of Paradise"—a fiscal assessment of the state written by various experts—hit the shelves, had since exploded. The price of gas was three times that of the mainland, and electric prices were the highest in the country. Many people worked two and three jobs just to pay their mortgage, while others had no home at all. Hawaii's huge homeless population was comprised of two types of people—those who had come there dreaming of black sand and palm trees but couldn't make ends meet, and those who were already homeless somewhere else and decided they wanted better weather.

They'd managed to scrounge up the plane fare, then spent their days begging for change and their nights camped on the beaches.

Many pundits contended that the state's political makeup was to blame. Hawaii was, and still is, about as blue as state can get—the last time it voted for a Republican president was Reagan in 1984, and state government has been almost exclusively run by Democrats ever since I could remember. The view was that the lack of opposing voices in government had led to a dearth of new ideas. While I saw their point, my thoughts ran to labor's role in the state's economic struggles. With more than 20% of its workforce belonging to one union or another, Hawaii had the third highest union density in the country, just behind New York and Alaska. Not coincidentally, construction costs were also exorbitant. As always happened when they had the numbers, labor leaders were unable to resist the temptation to take advantage; they would brag about the high rates they wrangled from the companies until they eventually priced themselves out of the market. Projects would run in fits and starts because employers didn't have the money to continue, and whenever they could, they hired nonunion workers. For all their chest-pounding and issuing of threats, they had succeeded only in shooting themselves—and their members—in the foot. Just thinking about it boiled my blood, and then I'd remind myself I was no longer in the labor game.

Chapter 15

My time at Starwood was the best time, professionally speaking, that I'd had in years. Unlike the International, it was a light-hearted environment with a staff who for the most part wanted me to be there. Ironically, it was also the place where I rediscovered my true purpose. As senior HR manager, I was in a position to liaise between workers and management in a way that was empowering to both. I taught them how to work with each other, and since there were no politics involved, I did so with a freedom I'd never enjoyed at the union. For the first time in a long time I could see the direct effects of my efforts on the people I served. Just six months later, though, I felt the pull of the union calling me back in.

It all started in the January of 2011, when I attended a meeting of Local 1260. Oddly enough, although the International had booted me from DC and maligned with potential employers, they had not bothered to revoke my union membership. I had not been to a local meeting in years, and now that I was back in Hawaii I had the urge to reconnect with the brothers. When I walked into the hall that night, I did not find the camaraderie of my youth, but a war zone. Five hundred guys were yelling and screaming, while Lance, Local 1260's business manager and the target of their ire—tried unsuccessfully to calm them down. From what I gathered, he had made some unpopular moves with regard to contract negotiations with Hawaiian Electric. It didn't help him any that he was up for reelection in a few months.

When they saw me, several people took a break from their yelling to come over and shake my hand. I didn't know how much they knew of the DC story, but they expressed happiness to see me before returning to the fray. I wasn't there long before I called Marilyn to come get me. "I don't want to stay here," I told her. "It's pure insanity."

When my brother-in-law, who worked for Hawaiian Electric, approached me soon after and asked me to run for business manager, I thought *he* was insane.

"No way. You were at that meeting—it's all screwed up. It will take an army to fix it."

Before long, other familiar voices joined the chorus. These were men I'd known for years, some since childhood, literally begging me to take the reins from Lance. Among them was Russell Takemoto, another employee of Hawaiian Electric who I had known for years. Every time I thought about it, I'd picture the chaos at the meeting, shake my head, and thank God I had the job at Starwood.

That didn't mean I had stopped caring about what went on in the union. One day I got a call from the CEO of one of the companies Local 1260 had an agreement with. I can't in good conscience name the company here; suffice it to say, negotiations between his team and Lance's had broken down, and he wanted my advice. I was, to put it mildly, shocked. It was one thing for a group of disillusioned members to think I could do something for them, and quite another to get a call from some random CEO I had never even met. I wondered who had given him my name and the idea that after all the years away I had something to offer.

I must be insane, I thought, even as I asked him to explain the situation. As much I wanted to be free of union politics, I could not divorce myself from the members. If I could do something to help them and didn't, I would always regret it.

After explaining some of the sticking points in the agreement, he said, "Off the record, Brian, Lance doesn't know what he is doing."

This came as no surprise; I'd heard as much at the members' meeting. Basically, it was the same old thing, with the union guys talking when they should be listening, fighting when they should be understanding, and demanding things that seemed important in the moment but would have little lasting impact. How, the CEO wanted to know, could he bridge the gap between the company's needs and Lance's "wish list"? This list was the things the union came to the negotiating table with and was usually based on complaints they'd heard from the members. The problem with this, I had found, was that it created a narrowness of mind that had no place when trying to come to a consensus. Instead of walking in the other guys' shoes, people with such a list tended to focus only on their own needs and wants.

I considered what he had told me about the agreement and decided that the company was indeed offering terms that would benefit the members.

"You have to lead them to it," I replied, "but in a subtle way. If they suspect you are trying to 'teach' them, they'll only dig their heels in more. You have to make them think whatever you're suggesting is their idea."

The CEO thanked me and took my advice back to his team. Though I never heard the particulars of future meetings, I did hear that the matter was resolved in a way that was best for both the members and the company.

At Easter, my brother-in-law cornered me again. As he spoke about the way things used to be at Local 1260 and how bad things had deteriorated in the years I'd been gone, I couldn't pretend I wasn't moved. Or fired up. Just the mention of the current state of the local and my mind was flooded with ideas as to how I could make it better. No matter what I had been through in DC, Local 1260 had always been a part of me, and I was not yet ready to cut it out.

As I debated what to do, I remembered a conversation I'd had with my parents back when my dad was sick, when I was about to move to the mainland as an International rep, which at the time was seen as a huge promotion. My parents and I had talked for a long time about God having a plan for all of us and that part of that plan was to make a positive contribution to the world; it was both a right and a responsibility. That day, I promised them that even though I was moving up in the union ranks, I would never forget where I had come from and that I would always come back and use my knowledge and experience to help the people of Hawaii. That conversation would serve as the tipping point in my decision.

I was finally convinced, but it didn't mean a thing unless Marilyn was on board. She had always and always would be my sounding board and the most honest person I know.

"Brian," she said when we sat down to discuss it, "are you sure you want to do this again, after everything you went through in DC?"

"Everyone is taking about it. They told me I can win, I can help change the culture."

I looked into Marilyn's eyes and could tell she thought it was a mistake; but I also knew that as always, she would support me 100 percent.

After declaring my intention to run, the first order of business was to quit Starwood to avoid any hint of a conflict of interest. This move was not taken lightly. I would have no income coming in, at least during the election process. As for what came later, well, I'd just have to roll the dice and see what happened.

Lance had been the business manager since 2008, and although people were dissatisfied with what he had done, he still had the power of incumbency behind him. He had access to union employees and members that I simply didn't have. Many of the people I knew from back in the day had since retired, and for the younger guys I was an unknown quantity. They could well decide to go with the devil they knew and then simply continue to complain.

There was plenty to complain about, not the least of which was the loss of the electric discount. This was a contract provision stating that employees of utility companies would get a 33% discount on their own bills. This would have been valuable anywhere, but in Hawaii, where the energy rates were the highest in the nation, it was sacrosanct. Then came Lance.

When it came to negotiations, Lance was a throwback to my father's day, but whereas my father would grandstand a bit in front of the members, he was much more even-keeled when sitting across the table from the company. For Lance, the idea of cultivating a relationship with companies was as outlandish as a fish with wings. Instead he built a wall that was impossible to transcend. "When I get in there I'm going to pound the table," he was fond of telling the members, "and we're going to get 10% or we're going to go on strike. They don't tell me; I tell them." Some called it old school; I called it archaic.

By the time he walked into those negotiations, the company already hated him. Over one hundred grievances piled up because he either couldn't or wouldn't resolve anything. Others he rushed to arbitration, which ran up the company's legal bills. He never cooperated with them, yet he had the gall to demand a 10 percent wage increase for the members. It was like punching someone in the face and then turning around and asking them for a favor.

Not surprisingly, the company said no to all of his demands. That's when Lance found himself in over his head. With no idea how to proceed, he figured he would buy himself some time by extending the contract from the end of October to the end of January. He didn't realize he had just given away all his power. The company said, "Sure, we'll extend it, as long as you sign away the electric discount."

A skillful negotiator knows that in order to arrive at the best possible agreement, one must leave their ego at the door. If they don't, they will either wind up giving away the farm or risk a complete breakdown in communication. This is why strikes have been so prevalent throughout labor history. Lance was so determined to wrest something from the company that he was willing to give up something as valuable as the electric discount.

Up to that point, however, all was not lost. The Public Utilities Commission (PUC), a state government agency charged with regulating and overseeing utility companies on behalf of the public, had ruled that the electric discount was no longer a recoverable item, meaning it was no longer a write-off for the company. As a safeguard, Local 1260 had a letter of agreement dated 1992, that if PUC ever tried to take the employee discount away, they would establish some sort of equivalency. When Lance signed that away, too, the members were incensed. Like anyone who had been in the union for decades, he still had loyal supporters. They even backed up Lance's claim that it was the International who had signed away their rights. Later, it was revealed that Lance's signature was indeed on the agreement; the International had nothing to do with it.

At the end of the day, an act of God would be the nail in Lance's coffin. Negotiations around the wage increase had all but broken down when on March 4, a terrible storm hit Hawaii. About fourteen thousand homes lost power, including most of Ewa Beach, an idyllic stretch on the southern tip of Oahu. During this crisis was when Lance decided to strike. Workers walked off the jobs as power lines were being repaired, leaving the company, and the public, at their mercy. Amid the public outcry and Governor Neil Abercrombie's condemnation of the strike, the IBEW put out a statement claiming that the timing was coincidental, but of course no one believed it. This was precisely the sort of thing that gave labor a bad name, and for good reason.

An opportunity often presented to labor unions, but one they rarely took advantage of, was of cooperation. Lance could have sent the line crews back to work to show the governor and the company they were willing to cooperate. The community would have been happy, and he would have been seen as a hero. Instead, he dug in his heels, for a while anyway. Everyone was out of work for a week, and in the end all Lance had to show for it was a paltry 1 percent wage increase. He had also managed to gamble away hard-won member benefits that had been in place since my father's day. Whereas they used to have a 100 percent Workman's Comp, they were now limited to the 66 2/3 percent mandated under state law. The vesting schedule for their medical contributions, which used to be a multitiered plan based on the length of their employment—five years, ten years, and so on—evaporated altogether. They now had to be with the company for a full twenty years before the provision kicked in.

During the ratification process, participating members asked Lance what the plan was should they decide to vote no. Would they stay on strike? Lance shrugged. "I don't know. This is the last, best, and final the company gave us."

I looked on, thoroughly disgusted. It is easy to go on strike; the hard thing is to have a plan to come out of it. At some point, the goal must be to get the members back to work and work things out with company. Lance had gone on strike with no plan, banking on the fact that the company would fold because of the storm.

With the election approaching in a few months, Lance found himself between a rock and a hard place. The contract was narrowly ratified, 600 to 550. His Neanderthal tactics had succeeded only in alienating the members, the company, and the public, and now I and the three other guys running were nipping at his heels. What was a nervous union boss to do? In true labor fashion, he set out to rid himself of the competition any way he could.

The IBEW constitution states that in order to run for office one must not only be a member of the union but also be working in a jurisdiction of the union. This makes perfect sense—they wanted someone with skin in the game, not just a casual member. Although my employment with Starwood did not fit this criteria, I wasn't worried, because Local 1260 did not have this provision in its bylaws. Besides, I'd had skin in this game since I was old enough to walk. That didn't stop Lance, though, who in March introduced the policy in a blatant attempt to have me removed from the ballot.

Blatant or not, per the rules his motion had to be read at the next board meeting. When I heard it had easily passed, I wasn't surprised. It was well known the board members were in the tank for Lance. Furious, I picked up the phone and called Mike Mowrey, then vice president of the Ninth District and a trusted friend. I told him my union membership was current until June and that Lance was trying to keep me off the ballot.

"If I lose this thing," I said, "it's gonna be because the members vote in someone else, not because of this nonsense."

Mike sighed. He, too, was weary of union games. "Okay, go ahead and file a complaint."

I did as he suggested, figuring it would go nowhere. A complaint would be kicked up to the International, which would then determine whether the suggested policy had merit. Considering my recent history, I was shocked when the International found that while the policy was indeed in concert with the constitution, the timing of it wreaked of impropriety. In other words, they knew Lance was being shady and didn't want it to blow back on them. I was allowed to remain on the ballot.

By the time election day rolled around, I was pretty sure Lance was going to lose, but that didn't mean I was going to win. Three other candidates were also running, and I had been gone a long time. My "campaign" had consisted mostly of calling up some people I knew from way back when and letting them know I was running. It paid off, though, for at the end of the day I won by forty votes, which was respectable for a five-man race.

Perhaps the most gratifying thing about winning was the phone call I received from a former colleague back in DC. Apparently a cheer had gone up in the office when people heard the news. After thanking my friend for the support, I hung up the phone and promptly burst into laughter. Oh, to be a fly on Ed Hill's office that day! He had so cleverly planned my ouster, but the one thing he had forgotten to do was revoke my union membership.

The results had no sooner been announced when Harold Dias whispered in my ear, "We'll bring Lance up on charges so he cannot run again. You'll have no competition next time."

"I'm not worried about competition," I told him. "I just want to do my job. I'll run again, and if I lose, then it wasn't meant to be."

Harold looked at me, completely nonplussed. "Why would you want to do that?" I later found out that Harold had encouraged Lance to sign that agreement with Hawaiian Electric that robbed the workers of their electric discount. Somehow, Lance had managed to get himself on Harold's hit list.

Here we go again.

Chapter 16

After my all-too-brief-respite at the Starwood, I once again found myself acclimating to a new political landscape. I understood that in his own way, Harold was trying to protect me; I just didn't know what he was protecting me from or, for that matter, why he cared. The first question was answered soon enough when Lance, in an apparent attempt to rid himself of competition at future elections, claimed that I had tampered with the one that had just passed. The fact that he, not I, had been in charge of facilitating the election made no difference; he just wanted to put a black mark on my record before I even took office. No matter how far-fetched the charge was, per the union rules it had to be checked out. As the International rep for the area, Harold Dias was charged with investigating it, then he would send his determination to Mike Mowrey, who in turn would send it to DC. They would all find the claim to be "frivolous and without merit."

By the time I was sworn in on July 1, I'd had enough of Lance's shenanigans, but the truth was they were little more than an annoyance. I was much more concerned with the attitude of the board members, who were fiercely loyal to Lance and furious that he had lost.

The swearing-in ceremony began as a joyous occasion; Marilyn came, and staff members brought me leis. Everyone smiled as if no one had expected anything other than victory. The true attitude of the board revealed itself when, shortly after I began speaking, they tried to cut the event short. It was one of the moments that you know will set the tone for an entire relationship; it is the moment when you let people know whether they can take advantage of you or not.

"Hold on," I said, holding up a hand, "I am not finished."

For the next hour, I spoke in detail about the things I wanted to accomplish during my three-year term. I pledged, first and foremost, that I would personally renegotiate all of Local 1260's contracts within that time, and that I would teach my staff to run negotiations without me. I also had plans to improve communication with members; resolve the long list of matters pending in arbitration and other grievances; and institute new training programs and ways to better utilize shop stewards. And that was just for starters. For the most part, people seemed enthusiastic about my plans; however, I had only to look at the faces of the board members to realize I had my work cut out for me.

I had been in office only a few weeks when Lance once again made his presence known, this time to file another equally ridiculous charge. I had not attended a membership meeting. No matter that nothing in the bylaws stated that the business manager or his staff had to attend such meetings, which were run by the chairman or the president. But I wasn't using technicalities as an excuse to shirk my duties. When issues came up, I would attend the meetings of various units to address the members' concerns directly; otherwise, I often felt my time was better spent on other matters that were again in service of the members. The complaint went through the process and received the same determination as the previous one: frivolous and without merit.

• • •

One of the things I'd hated most about the International was its façade of professionalism; the lovely office, the fancy suits, and clinking of Scotch glasses in high-end DC bars were all a cover for inefficiency and stagnant thinking. I'd spent six years longing for something authentic, a place where the work was more important than window dressing. Well, I was about to get my wish—tenfold. Local 1260 was the epitome of authentic. Back in 1993, my father had "renovated" the office—meaning he'd laid new tile and carpeting. Since then it had not been touched. The furniture was dilapidated and the paint peeling; I didn't want to know the source of the large, brownish stains on the carpet. It was, to use modern vernacular, a hot mess.

And that was just Local 1260's office. We rented out space in the building to United Food and Commercial Workers International (UFCW), a firefighters' union, and another IBEW local that represented telephone workers. Before the election a fire had broken out in the UFCW offices and spread through the entire building. Nearing the end of his term, Lance had decided to kick the can to his successor. So on top of my own work, I had to renovate the entire building, plus strip carpets.

I soon learned that aesthetics were the least of our concerns. The computers were from the last century, and the staff was still backing up their work on memory sticks, rather than database storage. Local 1260 had no website and no social media sites. Couple that with the reduced attendance at union meetings, and it added up to virtually no communication between the local and its members. I felt like I had walked into a time warp. Everywhere I looked, I got another reminder of labor's refusal to evolve with the rest of the world.

"What the hell happened while I was gone?" I asked, but no one seemed to have an answer.

Now topping the long list of things I wanted to accomplish as business manager was changing the public perception of Local 1260. Throughout my career—particularly in DC—I had seen seventy-year-old men trying to appeal to thirty-year-old workers, and failing miserably at it. They did not understand what the younger generations wanted, or how they thought. Gen-Xers and millennials had no experience with employers that made them work twenty-hour shifts or denied them health benefits; they had grown up in a time when much of their needs were protected by statute. To win them over, labor could no longer rely on pounding the table and fighting with companies; they would actually have to strategize. I, on the other hand, had observed the differences between the way my father had handled situations and the way I did, and Brandon often saw things differently altogether. It was a matter of seeing things from another's perspective, and bridging the gap.

I was also determined to change the way employers viewed us. I was well aware that some companies saw union guys as a bunch of uneducated goons, making demands without truly understanding the bargaining process or the concerns of management. As offensive as this description sounded, I could not blame them. We are all responsible for the image we project into the world, and most labor leaders behaved as though employers were fat cats to be taken for everything they had. I didn't care who had created or perpetuated that perception, it was going to end with me.

In addition, I also had an internal culture to shift. This would require me to do a little tightrope walking. My experience in DC, stifling as it was, had taught me a lot about the way to run an office, or rather how not to run it. Determined as I was to whip things into shape, I would not do it by harassing people who forgot to clock out. I would not force them to chain themselves to a desk or wear uncomfortable clothes. I was always most productive under my own power, and that's the environment I would create for my staff. People could wear shorts and flip-flops if they wanted, as long as they felt engaged in the work. For my part, this meant letting go of control and trusting that workers would rise to their potential. Ultimately, I would bear the responsibility for whatever they did.

As committed as I was to making these changes, I knew that without a strong foundation, my ideas would not be sustainable. It took only one glance around the dilapidated office to see that. I wanted to build a model that would be around long after I retired. The members had had enough lip service; now it was time for Local 1260 to deliver real, lasting results. This new model would be one that took labor to the future while honoring the ideals of its past. The motto would be "Every Member Matters," and it would be the guiding principle of every action I took while business manager.

The cornerstone of this model would be the people who implemented it. If I had learned anything throughout my years at the union, it was that nothing killed a dream faster than complacency and inertia. That said, I was bound by practical considerations, including the local's present financial state, so I decided to start off simple until I had everything figured out.

Even before the election I had begun vetting my team so if I won I could hit the ground running. One of the first people I reached out to was Russell Takemoto, a draftsman from Hawaiian Electric. I'd known Russell for years; in fact, while I was in DC he'd called me more than once to say I should return to Local 1260 because Lance "didn't know what he was doing." At the time I considered it idle gossip, but now I took it as an indication that Russell wanted to take Local 1260 in another direction. Also, though I had no need of a draftsman, I did need someone with contacts at Hawaiian Electric to serve as a member representative. He had no qualifications for this position, but I truly believed that with some time and grooming he could grow into it.

My other choices for representatives, Russell Yamanoha and Teresa Morrison, were equally unorthodox. Yamanoha had worked with Marilyn years earlier, when she was the executive assistant to the head of the television station and Russell was sports director for

Hawaii News Now. When I told Marilyn I needed a communications director to repair the image of Local 1260—particularly its members working at Hawaiian Electric—after Lance's infamous strike, she recommended Russell. I sat down with him and, after a short meeting, hired him as an at-will employee.

As for Teresa, I had only met her briefly more than a decade earlier, when she was a young college student working at the same after-school program as Marilyn. Teresa had impressed my wife and me as someone who was intelligent, ambitious, and committed to helping others. She was also from Pearl City and had graduated from my alma mater, Maryknoll. About a year before I got the International rep position, Teresa left for law school on the East Coast.

"Good luck in school," I told her. "I am going to look you up in the future because I think maybe you'll be able to help me with a program I will be building. This wasn't some sort of prophecy; it was 2002, before I had any inkling that I would be moving over to the International. I believed I would spend my career at Local 1260, and I had big plans for it.

A lot of water had flowed under the bridge since then, but shortly after declaring my intention to run for business manager, Teresa's name popped into my mind. I'd given a lot of thought to the type of staff I wanted to create—dynamic, creative, and committed—but in order to do that, certain barriers had to come down. While plenty of women had held administrative positions at Local 1260 over the years, they'd never had a female representative. They had also never had a full-time attorney on staff. Teresa, who had passed the bar and was practicing law on the mainland, filled both criteria. Shortly before the election, I called her up, and we had a productive discussion about how we could expand and rebrand Local 1260. When I won, I officially invited her to come on board.

Rounding out that core group were Local 1260's three veteran administrative assistants: Lorna Takahasi, Gay Yamafuji, and Leeann Miyamura. I didn't know Lorna and Gay all that well, but Leeann, another Pearl City native, was like family. We had known each other since grade school and still had many friends and acquaintances in common. When I asked her to stay on at Local 1260, I knew I would not have to explain my vision; she knew it because she knew me. It was a vision of empowering others toward self-determination by helping them to believe in their own value and purpose. Leeann knew the bylaws of Local 1260 and the constitution of the IBEW backward and forward, and I would count on her throughout my term to keep me versed and on message. As I stared at the mountain of work before us, I could only pray the others felt the same, and that it would be enough.

• • •

If someone had told me when I left DC that I would be running a local union, I would have laughed in their face. Now, scarcely a year later, I was standing in a burnt-out hovel, trying to figure out how I was going to fix it while dealing with limited funds and the miserly mob that held the purse strings. Yet somehow, instead of feeling overwhelmed, I found myself feeling more energized than I had in years. I'd had to travel all over the mainland to realize where I truly belonged: at Local 1260, directly impacting its members. One sentiment summed up my feelings: I felt like I was finally *home*.

Only one thing really broke my heart, and that was Guam. Winning the Raytheon campaign was still the proudest moment of my career, and those workers were especially dear to me. A few months after the election I flew down there to reconnect with them and their employers and get a read on the situation. The moment I stepped off the plane and into the thick, fragrant air, I felt as though I'd been transported back in time. The emotions I'd felt during the campaign nine years earlier—the passion, the anxiety, and ultimately the exhilaration—all came flooding back. To my delight, I was soon greeted by Pastor Ronocco, a local treasure who ministered to many of the workers. Though he was now approaching eighty, he didn't look that much older than he had when I'd last seen him.

"Brian, Brian," he said in his thick Filipino accent as he reached out to grip my hand, "I prayed every day that you would come back. Now my prayers have been answered."

I looked at him with some surprise. Prayed for me to come back? What the hell was going on down here? After I left Hawaii for the International rep position, another guy had been charged with taking care of things. Now I heard he hadn't gone down there *in years*. Raytheon was long gone, replaced by DZSP-21, an enormous company that provided base operation support—everything from maintenance and utilities to construction and food services—to the naval base. The company in turn subcontracted much of this work to three other companies, which meant that in addition to our main agreement, we had other contracts that had to be managed separately. The rep from Local 1260 had negotiated these contracts but never bothered to visit the workers—this, despite the fact that they represented *one third* of Local 1260's membership. This not only left them feeling like cast-offs but signaled a lack of union leadership to the companies. Even worse was the fiscal mismanagement. Guam generated $300,000 a year in union dues, but those workers saw none of the benefits. The money was instead siphoned to Hawaii and spent on God-knows-what there. I had to scratch my head on that one, because they certainly hadn't invested in the office. No wonder the membership had shrunk, from 1,003 when I left in 2003 to 700 when I returned nine years later. Some had lost their jobs as a result of downsizing, while others were simply tired of paying dues for nothing. It amounted to taxation without representation.

If I had any doubts that things were dire, they were erased when *five hundred* of those workers showed up at the members' meeting. I told them they had been taken for granted, but that was going to end right now. A collective groan went up from the crowd; they'd been discarded and lied to for years and thought I was feeding them another line of bull.

"For the first three years," I said, raising my voice above the din, "I will come every month for membership meetings. I will make sure you are being represented. There will also be a full-time rep with an office down here, and the door will always be open to hear your grievances. At the same time, we will continue to build a strong relationship with your employers."

Slowly, the room started to settle down. "There is one thing I ask, and that is that you allow me to skip the month of December so I can be with my family for the holidays."

At this, most nodded and said, "Sure, of course," while others groaned again and said, "Yeah, the last guy said he would come too, and he never showed."

I had done my best to reassure them with words, but the only way to truly silence the naysayers was with action.

Chapter 17

"I didn't leave the Democratic Party . . . the party left me."

A lifelong Democrat, I'd never been known to quote Ronald Reagan. Yet this statement, made by the Gipper in 1962, was spot-on when it came to my feelings about labor. My ideals had remained the same, but I no longer believed labor had the same ideals. The movement used to be bold and brave; it used to have a critical role in American society, but somewhere along the line it had abandoned that in favor of protecting its turf. Leaders focused on placating the 5% of members who made trouble, rather than uplifting the other 95%. It was the difference between true leadership and management: the former supports and empowers; the latter just breeds incompetency.

Determined as I was to change this, I knew I was in for one hell of a battle, particularly with the board of directors. Elected by the rank and file, the executive board consisted of eleven members, including four principal officers—the president, vice president, recording secretary, and treasurer—and several unit seats. Though I was now the head of the local, they had input in nearly every important decision, which was unfortunate, because more than half of them couldn't stand me. My crime? I had defeated Lance, to whom they were fiercely loyal. During my years in DC I'd almost forgotten that if anything, local unions were even more political than the International. These small fiefdoms had their own rules steeped in history and a labyrinth of complicated relationships, and the board was often at the center. Local 1260's board members were not motivated by money—they were paid a mere ten dollars for each meeting they attended—but by power, and they wielded it whenever they could. Unfortunately, they often did so without considering whether the action they were taking actually benefited anyone or simply punished someone they disfavored.

In my case, I think the board figured they would keep the status quo for three years until Lance could run again. From my first day on the job, they attempted to thwart my every move, from the miniscule to the major, and they did it primarily through their nearly absolute control of the purse strings. Although I was the business manager, per the union bylaws I could not spend a penny without their say-so. I could not even sign a check. The board took great satisfaction in denying every expenditure, regardless of the size of the purchase or the rationale behind it. I knew Local 1260 was far from flush, but the board's attitude went far beyond any sense of frugality. It was a power play.

I did have a few weapons in my own arsenal, however. When Lance was around, the board members used to knock back a few drinks during their meetings. I put a stop to that immediately. We were there to act on behalf of the members, I told them, and we would do so with clear heads. A few of them looked at me like I had stolen their puppies. "And no drinking before meetings, either," I added. If they didn't hate me before, they certainly did after that day.

Eventually I began making modest purchases and going to them for approval after the fact. When they refused to green-light a new television for the union hall—the one currently there had been given to my father by Hawaiian Electric more than two decades earlier—I headed over to Best Buy. Their reaction when I presented them with the bill for the television—an out-of-the-box special marked down from $500 to $399, was as expected: I was irresponsible, circumventing the process, et cetera, et cetera. I told them I respected their opinion, then announced they were not going anywhere until they approved the purchase. Under Local 1260's bylaws I could keep them there until eleven p.m., and I made sure every moment was as unpleasant as possible—with no air conditioning, no food, and worst of all, no drink. I then explained ad nauseum why it was sometimes necessary to spend money to make the union operate more efficiently, or simply to build the members' confidence. It was the labor's equivalent of the filibuster, and it worked. After awhile they were willing to approve the purchase of the Brooklyn Bridge if it meant they could get out of there and head over to the bar next door.

• • •

In their efforts to sabotage me, the board often took other, nonfinancial actions that were detrimental to the members.

A key piece of my plan to restore the members' confidence and revitalize the relationship with employers was the renegotiation of all of Local 1260's fifty-two contracts. While not all of them required an extensive overhaul, each provided an opportunity to strengthen existing relationships or cultivate new ones, and showed the members that the union was looking out for their interests. I believed—or hoped—that one day the two parties would not need an intermediary, and I suspected that day was coming sooner rather than later. In the meantime, I would build an environment of mutual trust and respect between them, for the benefit of both.

Each time I signed a new agreement or shook the hand of another employer, I felt like I was one step closer to my vision. Unfortunately, this also set me on a grueling pace that would almost be my undoing that first year. I soon found myself running around Hawaii, the mainland, and Guam.

True to my word, I hired Ken Laguana, a mild-mannered fifty-something, to serve as the full-time rep on the island. Ken was fairly green with regard to this type of work, but though his skillset was limited, I knew he had potential. He was starting to cultivate relationships with the members and the companies, and slowly but surely gained their respect.

I also kept my promise to get down to Guam each month. I would leave on a Monday night, and between the eight-hour flight and the eight-hour time difference, arrive on Tuesday night. I spent Wednesdays and Thursdays meeting with Ken, the companies, and the members to listen to any grievances they had. On Friday, I would take a six thirty a.m. flight, only to get back to Hawaii on *Thursday* night. Given all the travel I was doing, I often woke up wondering where

I was, but nothing was as disorienting as the strange, time-twisting travel between Guam and Hawaii.

Everyone kept telling me to slow down, including Marilyn, even though she knew better than anyone that I would not listen. A hundred ideas had percolated in my mind for years, and I did not want them to fall by the wayside. My staff soon tired of my endless texts and emails: Let's put this into place, how can we do this, let's put together a small team to . . . How do we build a construction site? How can we change the financial structure so that we can take care of members if financial actions need to be taken with an employer? How can we create a space for members to socialize, go out into the community? How can I formulate good partnerships? How can we be more politically active, on a local and national level? The list went on and on.

As business manager, it was incumbent upon me to understand all of Local 1260's contracts. Organizing is the lifeblood of the union; like any enterprise, if it is not growing, it is shrinking. That said, it is only part of the equation. To truly facilitate growth, one could not just stop with bringing a group of workers into the union, as this would eventually breed feelings of neglect and disillusionment. My father had taught me the importance of having a "soup-to-nuts" understanding of every relationship with workers. In other words, not only run the organizing campaign but negotiate the contract, get it ratified, and actively service it. In this way you provide continuity to members and avoid the degraded situation I'd found in Guam. As I came up the ranks of the union, representing members in the various capacities of shop steward, rep, and organizer, I had witnessed the wisdom of these teachings. Harry, who was my father's successor, didn't understand the Service Contract Act; he only understood utilities. The same was true of Lance. His goal, conscious or not, was to limit Local 1260 to its agreements with Hawaiian Electric, Maui Electric, KIUC, and Hawaii Electric Light Company. He would neglect other jurisdictions as if waiting either for the workers to decertify (leave the union) or for the International to create a separate local altogether. Then election time would roll around and Lance would try to curry favor with the members in order to get the votes. The members weren't stupid, though, which was why they had voted him out. Relationships with both the employees and employers, some of them going back decades, now had to be rebuilt, and thanks to my lengthy background with the union, I was in a unique position to do it.

Unfortunately, my staff could not provide this continuity. While some of it had to do with their lack of follow-through, the fact was they simply didn't have my history with the union. Having my father as a resource had proved invaluable long after he was gone. I remembered many things not just from having read a contract but by being there during its ratification. When someone asked me a question about a particular aspect of an agreement, I could tell them, "In 1973, this happened. Go into the letters of agreement and you will see a page, 'Contracting of work.' You will find a letter signed by my dad." I would then tell them to go to a particular section of a particular article, where they would find the answer to their question.

A few months in, exhaustion had become my closest companion. I had always been a workaholic. Even in DC I often went in early and stayed late; I sometimes even went in on Saturdays to finish up one report or another. But I had never kept a schedule this grueling. If not for the shortness of breath, I probably wouldn't have noticed how generally crappy I felt. When I finally went to the doctor, she announced that I had pneumonia and should be in bed.

I shook my head. "No, Doc. Just give me something so I can keep working. I have a pretty green staff and I need to show up. The membership is counting on me."

She didn't say anything else as she handed me a prescription for antibiotics, but her look said it all. She thought I was nuts, and I was starting to agree with her.

• • •

Thankfully, Local 1260's most important negotiations would take place close to home. We had another year to go on our existing contract with Hawaiian Electric, but management had agreed to open it up earlier—a gesture I took as a sign of trust in our relationship. It was also perfect timing for both the company and the union to renegotiate the agreement. One of the first things I'd done after taking office was sit down with Governor Abercrombie and assure him that I would never call a strike during a storm. It was a day late and a dollar short for the community, though; a year after Lance called that strike during the storm, public approval of both parties was still at an all-time low. Announcing a new alliance between Local 1260 and the company would hopefully go a long way to appeasing the thousands who had been left without power.

I had my own reasons for wanting to sit down with the company. I wanted to tweak several items in the contract, either because they were outdated or ran counter to what I wanted to accomplish. For example, I was highly concerned by the effect technology would have on our members, particularly around energy. At that time, Hawaii was a leader in renewable energy; it also had aggressive goals moving forward—meaning by 2045 it would have to be operating on 100% renewable energy. What would happen to workers whose jobs were made obsolete in the process? As it was, meter readers were already being told to look for other jobs. I wanted to proactively get a handle on the situation and eventually get a promise from the president of the company that these workers would be retrained in other areas. This strategy was known as "bargaining to organize," and was highly effective in increasing—and protecting—union membership by working within an existing contract rather than waging an expensive, time-consuming campaign.

As I had stated when taking office, one of my goals was to train the staff in the negotiating process so they could eventually handle it on their own. We took suggestions from the members, then brought them to the company, which had its own proposal. We then began the tedious, sometimes tense process of going through each document line by line to see if we could come to a happy medium. We would utilize "mutual gains bargaining," meaning we would discuss interests and issues only, with none of the bartering or horse trading typical of labor negotiations. Over a three-month period, I would cycle about one hundred people to participate in the talks.

At that time, the biggest issue was Hawaiian Electric's call center representatives, who were getting paid a whopping forty dollars an hour (roughly $80,000 a year straight time and as much as $150,000 with overtime). This was just for answering the phones; they actually became angry when they were asked to do anything extra, such as trying to "upsell" customers during such calls. They argued that they were making an "average" salary. This was certainly news to me; according to my research, most call center reps across the country made just fifteen to twenty dollars an hour. These bloated wages were ultimately absorbed by the community—Hawaiians paid the highest electric rates in the nation—and prevented the company from hiring more workers. We were also pricing ourselves out of the market and ultimately hurting the union. At first, the members didn't want to hear about the big picture; they just wanted to know their wages would be protected now.

It was a familiar scenario, repeated time and again over the decades. Back in 1987, when most labor leaders were still banging their fists on the table for low-hanging fruit, my father had come up with a level wage structure at Hawaiian Electric. He knew that getting small wage increases of 3, 4, or 5 percent would appease the members in the moment but were unsustainable in the long term. Eventually, the janitor and the mail clerk would be making forty to fifty dollars an hour, well above the company's means. What would happen to the members then? It was then that he created tiers for incoming employees. It was the same thing I wanted to do with the call center. It would help Hawaiian Electric sustain itself and allow them to go before PUC and tell them they had negotiated with the union and were competitive.

Faced with the members' skepticism, I turned to the company to see what headway I could make there. They, too, had had their fill of the old-school union guys, those who came in and made demands as if the company owed them something. They were shocked when I went in there and said things like, "Let's talk about your profit margin," and "What do you consider a fair rate increase?" then actually listened to the answers. Of course, I had already done my research, and knew, for example, how much a 3% raise would affect the company's productivity and its bottom line. Even after they had finished speaking, I did not demand anything. I simply explained how what I was proposing would benefit both the union and the company.

That proposal created a two-tier system of wages. Those currently at the call center would stay at their present rate, but moving forward, new hires would be paid 10 percent less. This protected loyal employees and promised a respectable thirty-five dollars an hour for future generations, while also honoring the company's interests. It was a win-win for everyone.

• • •

The call center was only part of the agreement, however. It also included a 25 percent increase, across all of the islands, over five years, thereby bringing the wages for journeymen—a catch-all term for a skilled worker who has completed an official apprenticeship program in a building trade or craft—and linemen up to the West Coast standard. The new agreement also encompassed other benefits as well. Back in 1998, I had recalculated pension so that members could take $50,000 in a lump sum to pay off bills. Now, I got Hawaiian Electric to double that amount; plus the members would still receive a monthly benefit check. When the company expressed reservations, I explained that under the Employment Retirement Income Security Act (ERISA), the pension was fully funded, so there was no risk to them.

At the end of the negotiations, I left feeling proud of what had been accomplished, not by me, but by the entire team on both sides. We had come to a beautiful agreement, and one I was confident the members would ratify.

Of course, some people complained; they were the same people who could not or would not see the forest for the trees. They never thought of how something might benefit them in the future, let alone what it might mean for others. It was one of those times that I had to remind myself to remain calm. After months of painstaking work on their behalf, it was frustrating when members scoffed at the result.

"What if the rate is too low?" one guy, a Lance supporter, shouted out after I had finished explaining about the call center.

I bit back a retort and said, "I'm sure plenty of people would be very happy to make thirty-five dollars an hour. Of course, anyone who thinks that's too low is free to take employment somewhere else."

Others took issue with the fact that the wage increase for journeymen would happen over five years.

"I wanted to lock them into a long-term agreement," I explained, "not to allow the dust to settle, but to bring stability for you folks."

"This all sounds good," yet another guy shouted, "but where are the takeaways?"

Takeaways were concessions, things we would have had to give up in order to get the benefits I had just described. The members were so used to getting screwed over, they could not wrap their minds around an excellent deal.

"What you are holding in your hands is the complete and final agreement between Local 1260 and Hawaiian Electric," I replied. "You can either ratify or reject it."

At the end of the day, the members overwhelmingly voted to ratify the new contract. The 10 percent decrease for new call center employees spurred Hawaiian Electric to hire sixty additional workers, and the applicants showed up in droves.

I later found out that before the vote, several of the board members had gone around to the various companies, trying to convince workers *not to ratify* it. Clearly, if I wanted to accomplish my goals, something had to be done about the board.

It turned out I didn't have to do anything. One day, seven of them abruptly quit. They also put out a statement to the members, announcing that they were leaving because they could not work with me, apparently because *I didn't know what I was doing.*

The statement ended with a call to action: "Follow us. Come to the next membership meeting."

No one came.

Aside from the election itself, it was the biggest indicator that Local 1260 was finally starting to move in the right direction.

Chapter 18

Ironically, after a year of trying to get in my way, the board members caused the most damage when they walked out. My first thought—sheer joy that they were gone—was quickly followed by the realization that they had left me without a quorum, or the minimum number of members needed to take valid action. When I took office there had been eleven board members, as stated in Local 1260's bylaws; however, I had fought—and won—to add two more seats so that Guam would also be represented on the board. This was a huge victory, but it also meant I needed seven people for a quorum. I now had six, and as the president and the treasurer were among the defectors, I could not issue any checks. I could not pay the electric bill, the cable, or the wages. I was dead in the water.

"Just hang in there," I told my anxious staff, "while I figure this out."

Even as I said the words, I wondered how I was going to accomplish this. Without a quorum I could not even fill the empty seats on the board!

Now I was left with the question of what constituted a quorum: a portion of the total number of board seats, or the total present? For the second time since leaving the International, I reluctantly turned to Ed Hill for assistance. Though he had found in my favor when Lance tried to keep me off the ballot, I knew he was still reeling from my win and would likely rule against me. Thankfully, Ed took the position that we could establish a quorum based on the number of people currently on the board. This meant I only need four of the six people. I had no idea why Hill did this for me; I could only assume it was somehow in his own interest. In any event, I was too grateful to think about it.

As business manager I could not unilaterally fill a board position; that said, my recommendation held a fair amount of weight, and my first recommendation was Kris Hoke for president. Once she was voted in, I handed her a list of names of people I trusted for vice president, recording secretary, and treasurer. They were quickly approved, and just like that, I had a board that understood what I was trying to do for Local 1260. After more than a year in office, I felt like I was finally in business.

• • •

As if I didn't have enough on my plate that first year, I also found myself pulled into the various political squabbles running rampant in Local 1260. Many of them predated my return; others were simply part of the grease that had always oiled the labor machine. Later, I would realize it was naïve to think I could stay out of them complete-ly. All I could do was hold true to my commitment to the members and try to let the other stuff roll of my back.

It seemed that everywhere I turned, someone was angling for something and expected me to either deliver or roll over and let them have their way. Almost immediately, members of my staff formed alliances and grudges in equal measure. Perhaps the most unlikely friendship was the one that sprung up between Tommy Decano and Teresa Morrison. Tommy was the stereotypical union dinosaur—a tough guy in his sixties who was rough around the edges; Teresa was a well-travelled attorney and young enough to be his daughter. Teresa had the intelligence, willingness, and drive to do the job; Tommy did not know how to use a computer. Yet they undeniably had some sort of bond. More than once I found Teresa doing Tommy's reports instead of her own and pointed out that the members were paying two salaries for a reason.

If the two of them weren't whispering conspiratorially, they were coming to me to suggest that so-and-so should be fired or that I should give them—Tommy and Teresa, that is—promotions, raises, or some other benefit. Mostly, they complained that the Russells did not know what they were doing. I conceded that point—to do otherwise would have made me look like I had my head in the sand—then reminded them that this was a rookie staff and we were still in the process of building our model. This was the time to be focusing 100 percent of our energy on *doing our jobs*, rather than complaining about others. The same was true when the other staff members badmouthed Lance.

"We have to work with what we were given and move on," I'd tell them, "not harp on what already happened."

Easier said than done.

I tasked Tommy with negotiating our contract with Davey Tree, a multinational tree-trimming company with a location on Oahu. In addition to its work on private properties, Davey did line clearance for the utility company, meaning they trimmed branches so they would not interfere with the power lines. This utility work fell under Local 1260's purview.

At the time, Teresa and I were tied up with a court case with the Department of Labor. I kept waiting for Tommy to sit down with Davey, but he refused to do it by himself. When the court case wrapped, Teresa and I negotiated the contract, then Teresa put together the ratification proposal, which would be voted on by the members at a meeting a few days later. Only then, at this critical moment, did Tommy decide to take the lead. Teresa and I arrived at the meeting to find that the vote had already happened, and not in our favor. Tommy had gotten there early, waved the sign-in sheet and ratification sheet at the members, and said, "You're stupid if you vote no."

In doing this, he was not only doing a disservice to our members, but violating a legal obligation to the company. Whenever the union came to a tentative agreement, we signed a document promising to endorse the deal to ensure a winning vote. Sometimes an agreement was on its face favorable to the members and ratified without a hitch. But more often than not, we had to explain certain aspects and even "sell" to the rank and file. This could be anything from a wage rate that increased in smaller-than-desired increments; different tiers of wages based on when one was hired; or, as in the case of Davey, the time frame for the creation of a full-fledged apprenticeship program.

The members wanted to hear that this program would be up and running "yesterday," which would have been impossible. Programs of that nature take a couple of years to implement, mostly due to the red tape associated with becoming accredited in the state of Hawaii. The members didn't want to hear about red tape; to them, it the term is a euphemism for "never gonna happen," then the union, the company, or both were screwing them over.

This is in no way meant to disparage the intelligence of the rank and file. These agreements were often complicated and had long-term ramifications understood only by those who sat in on the negotiations, hence the need for some finessing at the members' meeting. It's not that a journeyman could not grasp the ins and outs of a contract, should he so choose, but if he is a union member, he shouldn't have to! That's why he paid his union dues, to be represented by people versed in labor laws who had a body of knowledge about the particular jurisdiction (i.e. construction, utilities, et cetera) and had done the research and built a relationship with the employer they were dealing with. This was—and still is—one bone of contention I have with labor. Many labor guys, especially those of the old school, think their job begins and ends with strong-arming the big, bad company, then bragging to the members about it. This would be bad enough if the resulting agreements were optimal for the members, but this is usually not the case. Instead, union negotiators would demand low-hanging fruit and rarely took into account potential changes to the industry or other variables that might impact workers going forward. They were, in essence, trading long-term security and growth for instant gratification, while those on the company side calculated their bottom line for years to come, probably laughing about labor's shortsightedness. Over the years I had seen plenty of people, from the lowest rung of the union to the president himself, handle things this way. My predecessor Lance was a prime example; his idea of a ringing endorsement would be to give a cursory explanation of a contract to the members, then say, "I don't know, it's up to you folks." This was part of the reason the relationships between Local 1260 and the companies had degraded during his time in office.

There were of course those—my father chief among them—who were quite skilled at bridging the gap between the members and their employers. Fortunately for me, I'd had years to observe those who knew what they were doing and those who didn't, and I had learned from both. When I brought a contract to a meeting for ratification, I prepared a PowerPoint presentation that translated the legalese of the documents into plain English. Sometimes I also gave members a three- or four-page handout with the salient points. During the presentation I would fully explain what had occurred during the negotiations, then give the members an opportunity to ask additional questions. Only after all their concerns had been addressed would we put it to a vote. I had used this method with all of our Hawaiian Electric and Pacific Missile Range contracts, and each time it had worked wonderfully. The members felt empowered because they were voting for something they understood; moreover, they appreciated the fact that the union respected them enough to explain the terms to them.

After that first meeting, I gave Tommy one more chance to convince the members to ratify the contract with Davey, and he was again unsuccessful. On the third try, I sent Teresa instead, and she did a good job of explaining the logistics, convincing them that it was a priority for Local 1260. The members were still not thrilled about waiting so long for the apprenticeship program, but the message hit home. The contract was ratified by a close margin.

Aside from Teresa, Tommy was not shy about letting people know when they got under his skin. Part of his duty was to oversee Ken Laguana, the rep down in Guam.

He was not, however, any closer to getting Ken's respect. The two spoke three to five times a week, and Tommy went down to Guam once a month to check up on things. Russell Yamanoha happened to accompany him on one such trip, and the two borrowed Ken's car for the day, presumably to take care of business. As they sped along the highway, Yamanoha said, pointing to their empty food containers and other trash scattered about, "We have to clear out the car before we give it back to Ken."

Tommy glanced over at him. "Oh yeah, and why is that?" And with that, he took the trash and threw it out the window.

I never knew what poor Ken had done to get on Tommy's bad side, but I'd heard that Tommy often called him a "fat fuck" or "dumb ass," even when other people were around.

One day, Ken had finally had enough. When Tommy started berating him while driving down the highway, Ken promptly pulled over to the side of the road and told him to get out.

• • •

While I found most of these distractions frustrating, some were downright amusing. In 2012, I reintroduced Lance's proposal that one must be working under an IBEW jurisdiction in order to run for office. Its most outspoken opponent? Lance himself! This, despite that the proposal used the same exact language. Apparently it wasn't as appealing when not used to ice out someone weeks before an election.

In those early days, Harold Dias often acted as my ally; however, I would soon learn that I was expected to reciprocate tenfold. In fact, he may have been the biggest political operator in my world. Back in 1998, Harold had served as business manager of Local 1357. In his five years in office, membership dropped from 2800 members to 700, and the coffers dipped from over $1,000,000 to around $200,000. His mindset had been to get as much money as he could for the members; the problem was that he succeeded only in pricing them right out of the union. The company used a subcontractor, and Harold, thanks to his political maneuvering, was rewarded with an appointment to the International staff. He was completely motivated by self-interest, a fact I should have kept in mind when he was going to bat for me. With Harold, there was always a price.

Shortly after taking office, I got a call from the head of NLRB in the Pacific region. We had known each other for the better part of twenty-five years, and after we made the usual niceties, he got down to the point of the call. He needed a favor. A union member who had lost his job in 2007 had been lobbying ever since to get it back.

"This guy is giving me such a hard time, Brian. Can you just take the case to arbitration and settle it? That way if he loses, then he cannot come back and bother me anymore."

As soon as he said the man's name, I knew exactly who he was talking about. In fact, I'd already read through the case and told the worker he didn't have a leg to stand on. He hadn't been cheated or mistreated, but fired for cause. But this guy hadn't let the matter drop in five years and he wasn't about to now. That meant I had no choice but to weigh two costly options.

On the one hand, I couldn't see spending the members' money— roughly $40,000 for the union's share of the arbitrator, court reporter, and attorney's fees—on an unwinnable case. On the other hand, if I did nothing and he chose to sue the union for not properly representing him, Local 1260 would wind up shelling out $100,000 for lawyers and court costs. I hadn't been involved that long, but I had the distinct impression he might well be headed for a lawsuit. It was a crap shoot.

"I have to think about this," I told the NLRB head, which he seemed to accept.

Harold Dias was a different story. The fired employee had apparently been calling him as well, and dealing with him had started to feel disturbingly like work. That's why he became Int'l rep for Kauai when all the work was on Oahu.

"This guy has been calling me up," Harold said, "bugging me for the last three weeks. Brian, can't you just take the case?"

"But Harold, it's a loser." I then reiterated my concerns that I would be wasting members' money on a case that was by all accounts frivolous and without merit.

"Brian, I would highly recommend that you take it."

I didn't like the tone creeping into his voice. "And why would you highly recommend I take it, Harold?"

"Let's just say it would be in your best interests."

I wanted to ask him why this mess was being lumped on my plate. The guy had been fired years ago, when I was in DC, so why hadn't it been resolved then? I would never have the answer, but I did know that Harold wanted this thing put to bed as quickly and quietly as possible; he didn't want to have to put anything in a report that would lead to investigation, especially if it meant he would have to side with me in writing. Depending on which way the political winds were blowing, it could come back to bite him in the ass. I was well aware of the way things worked, and I accepted it as part of union life. What I took issue with was that Harold thought he could strong-arm me. He was sadly mistaken. After telling him he would have my decision soon, I hung up the phone.

As I looked through the case again, I felt the frustration building, not with the NLRB head or even Harold, but with the employee. Had he been wronged, I would have done anything to make him whole, but this guy had screwed up at work and was just looking for a payday. My hands were tied.

As costly as it was, I eventually decided to go with arbitration. A lost case there would in effect end the worker's campaign to get his job back. While he wouldn't technically be barred from bringing suit against the union, he would have a hell of a time finding an attorney to take his case. An attorney would ask him a series of questions: Were you under a union contract? He was. Didn't you go and see you union? He did. Did you go through arbitration process and if so, what was the outcome? Yes, he did and he lost. After that no lawyer would touch it. As disgusted as I was that I had to spend good money just to shut him up, I eventually decided to go with arbitration. To avoid any conflict of interest, I hired an outside attorney. I could almost hear Harold gloating over my decision, but I hadn't done it for him, I had done it for the members.

Chapter 19

"The decision to join or not join a service union, political party or other organization should be left up to the individual. No such organization has the right to take money out of the pockets of state workers without their proper consent." This statement, made by former Missouri Governor Matt Blunt, was not a cry in the dark; in fact, it reflected a growing sentiment across the country that labor, once a champion against abuses of power, had become the abusers.

In 2012, a few years after Blunt left office, the Supreme Court echoed this sentiment when it decided *Knox et al. v. Service Employees International Union, Local 1000*. The union had imposed a midyear union dues increase in order to fight what it considered to be antiunion initiatives on the California ballot, and it did not give employees an opportunity to opt out. The workers, who were not members of the union, contended that the dues were in effect a violation of their First Amendment rights, as they were forced to pay for political activities they did not agree with. Local 1000 argued that they must be able to assess such fees in an "emergency" so they could fight for workers as the need arose—in this case, before these ballots were voted on. As mentioned earlier, the Abood case in the 1970s had determined that public unions could charge nonunion members for activities related to collective bargaining, but only if they were nonpolitical. In SEIU the court took the Abood decision a step further and stated that nonmembers must give their affirmative consent to be charged for such activities. In other words, an opt-out opportunity was no longer sufficient; workers had to *opt in*.

The decision sent waves of outrage throughout the labor world, of course. Leaders and those supporting them hurled all the usual accusations—the court was "pro-business and anti-worker"; they had intentionally tied the unions' hands, which was akin to stripping workers of representation. Others, however, applauded the decision as one supportive of the individual's right to self-determination. Workers should not have to sacrifice their personal political beliefs in order to be represented by the union.

I often wondered whether I was the only union boss who agreed with the court. Workers needed strong, decisive leaders confident in their abilities to act on behalf of the whole. That said, I also believed that each person has the capacity and the right to judge what's best for him or herself, particularly when it comes to political beliefs. Power may be in numbers, but each member must first be empowered with knowledge and a voice before he can become part of a movement. At Local 1260 we had a political fund, usually to support a prounion candidate or some measure we believed would benefit the members. Each year our auditor would come up with the percentage of dues that could be contributed to political activities, then staff members would give x amount out of each paycheck. Other locals did it a little differently, assessing five cents an hour for each member of the union.

These contributions were all voluntary; the irony was that the unions had to be forced into this by the Supreme Court.

Personal choice was a core tenet of the model I was building, and just one of the areas in which I broke with the labor establishment. Another was the perception of corporations. Although I had lived my entire life in the union, I'd never shared my comrades' disdain for employers. In fact, I always liked to think I'd kept a foot planted firmly in the business world. Even back in the days before DC, when I still believed labor was making a positive impact on workers, I made it my business to keep up with trends in various industries, including the way companies invested their money and increased productivity. This knowledge would become an integral part of the model I was creating at Local 1260. Whereas labor continued to cling to the old mentality—that employers were diametrically opposed to unions and cared only about their bottom line—I disagreed. Unions had their bottom line, too—the union dues they collected—and as much as I hated to admit it, I suspected that they cared just as much if not more than the companies. Oftentimes, companies were willing to risk their bottom line temporarily in order to grow and assure sustainability in the long term. Most labor leaders, on the other hand, refused to part with a dollar even if it would further their cause, and if anyone suggested an out-of-the-box idea to spur growth, they were immediately shut down. This way of thinking had led to the slow but steady decline in membership nationwide. I was determined to incorporate positive aspects of both the labor and the business worlds into Local 1260, and if it did not work, at least I would know that I had not participated in the complacency.

On the union side, I drew from the rich history of being committed to a movement. Though by now I believed that labor leaders had lost their way, I knew in my heart that the camaraderie I had seen in that union hall as a kid was real. Those men, though rough around the edges and not all that worldly, had the wisdom that comes from knowing what is truly important in life—family, friends, God, and having a purpose in life. My father, while a man of rare conviction and strength, was not the only man of his generation to truly be dedicated to the professional and personal lives of the members. Since his retirement, things had fallen by the wayside, but I still remembered everything he had taught me, and my intention was to take those lessons and build a local that was a force for good, not just for its members, but for employers and the community in general. Whether they articulated it or even realized it themselves, I knew that in this fast-paced, tech-dependent world, people were hungrier than ever for personal contact.

Other aspects of the model would be based on a corporate paradigm, or at least the paradigm of the future. For years, companies had been shifting away from the old culture—where the boss had to have eyes on their employees at all times—and toward a more mobile, trust-based model. Telecommuting was on the rise; according to one study I read it had increased 79% between 2005 and 2012. It allowed people the opportunity to spread their wings and save money and time on commuting. It also saved companies enormous sums in overhead. There was no hard and fast rule—each organization had to find a system that worked for them. Some businesses did not even have a central office at all.

Like any other organization, I vetted my staff for a few months to assess their strengths and challenges. Then, I told most of them that they could work remotely.

"Come to the office when you need to," I told them, "not just to show your face." I didn't care if they showed up at ten and left at one, so long as they were working. In fact, I actually preferred them to be at the various plants, listening to the members' grievances and figuring out how to address them. Our whole purpose of being there was to be visible and accessible to those who paid their union dues with their hard-earned money. We had to earn it as well. For the most part, labor did not understand this mentality. Sure, they spouted the rhetoric about fighting the oppression of the American worker, but that was only when employers were the ones doing the so-called oppressing.

• • •

After more than a year of fighting with the original executive board, I felt like an enormous boulder had been removed from my path. Despite the aggravation, I'd been reminded that for all my travels, Local 1260—and its members—was my home and my heart, and I was now in a position to affect them directly.

In order to get anything accomplished, I would first have to dive into the financial quagmire I'd been left with. When I came on board, the union had only $500,000 in the coffers, which was a bit odd, considering how tight-fisted the previous board had been. While it was always a goal to increase membership and therefore dues, that would not be enough to change the big picture. My plan was to provide new opportunities for the members to bond, not only with each other but with the larger community, as well as to have access to vocational training that would allow them to advance in their careers or even change them. In other words, Local 1260 had to offer workers something other than an incremental raise. Clearly, a more drastic move was needed, something that would catapult us to a different level and allow us to change, not just our present circumstances, but to ensure sustainability for the future. Like most "radical" solutions, it had been staring everyone in the face. It was time to get into the real estate business.

In and of itself, Local 1260's dilapidated old union hall wasn't worth much, especially since Lance had taken out an $80,000 loan against it. This made little difference to me, though, because in Hawaii, the land is what counts, and the plot our building sat on had been assessed at over $5 million. I engaged a commercial realtor, and before I knew it the Honolulu Credit Union expressed interest in the property.

I arrived at the next board meeting with a meticulously crafted plan. I would need all the executive officers' signatures for the sale, and though they were in my corner, they would still need convincing proof. The money from the sale would allow us to completely change the financial structure—and future—of the local. We could purchase properties for meetings, and recreational retreats for the members. I also planned to hire Outer Island reps—one stationed on each island of Hawaii—so members would no longer have to wait for someone to fly out to them.

Had the old board still been in place, this change would have been unthinkable; they would have refused to approve the sale no matter what case I made or how long I kept them in the room. Kris Hoke and the others, however, immediately saw the potential gains, and with a 5 to 0 vote gave me the green light for the sale of the hall and the purchase of one property; any subsequent purchases would have to be approved separately. The request was then kicked up to the International, where Ed Hill surprised me once again with his approval. Oddly, the man who had thrown up so many roadblocks when I was working for him had done nothing but clear the way since I'd taken office. Shortly thereafter, the credit union purchased the property for $5.4 million. It was the largest sale in the history of the area.

The board also approved my request to lease our new office space. I was determined to find something that would encourage business-es and philanthropic organizations to see us as equals. The Topa Building, located in downtown Honolulu, was the perfect fit. The offices on the sixteenth floor were large, with an incredible view of the Pacific. They also had fluorescent lighting and stained rugs. It seemed that if there was a rundown hovel anywhere in the state of

Hawaii, it ended up in the hands of Local 1260. I didn't mind, though; in fact, it was energizing to make it our own. We bought new furniture and computers; we laid down new carpeting and erected partitions, and when it was finished, it was an airy, open space worthy of any corporate office.

As I decorated my own office, I couldn't deny the feeling of pride over what we had built in such a short time. On the wall, I hung a picture of Jimmy Hoffa, a choice I knew some people would consider odd. They could think what they wanted, but I would argue that they didn't know the whole story. Hoffa had a great passion for organized labor; he'd stood firmly on the side of the working man and understood that organizing was the lifeblood of the labor movement. The fact that he had eventually lost his way did not change that. His picture served not as an endorsement of his faults, but a reminder of all he had achieved, and that the rest of us must stay the course even when we were disillusioned.

Though I had the approval for it, I did not rush to purchase another property, but opted to let the money grow. Lee Financial, a company that worked with Goldman Sachs, Deutsche Bank, and Cantor Fitzgerald, put $3,000,000 into relatively low-risk investment funds. One of the notes was directly tied to the Dow Jones Industrials, which grew by nearly 2500 points from the time of investment to the day I was removed from office.

● ● ●

Anyone from a mainland local would have been jealous to hear of Local 1260's beach house on the Big Island. That is, unless they actually saw it. The two-story building hadn't been touched since the mid-80s, when I joined my father and some of the other guys to lay down peel-n-stick tiles and fix the glass doors. Dad had also closed down the upstairs, and now, as I climbed the stairs, I could smell the heavy, rancid stench. The bodies of dead rats in various stages of decay littered the floor. They had crawled into the rafters from the coconut tree outside and then were unable to get back out. The bill for the renovations was a cool $50,000, but well worth it. The house could now be rented to members for a nominal cleaning fee of fifty, maybe a hundred bucks. The upstairs would later become the office for Big Island's Outer Island rep. I dedicated it to my father.

With our coffers growing and two successful renovations under our belt, I finally headed to Kauai to look for a house similar to the one on the Big Island. When I showed the pictures of my first choice to the board, they nodded and said, "We trust you, Brian." Simple words that in the union world were extremely hard to come by, especially when the people uttering them were willing to put money—in this case, $700,000—behind it. Ed Hill also gave his approval without incident. Now all that was left to do was break the bad news to my staff.

"For the first two years," I told them, "we cannot rent it. This is for the members and the members only. I don't want anyone thinking that this is some kind of perk for us." I held my hand up to silence the groans. "You can go if one of the members has a function there. Then, after two years, we'll revisit the issue of our renting it."

This was not about being tough on my own staff, but about reminding everyone that we were there to enrich the members, not ourselves. One of the things I missed most about the union of my childhood was the social aspect. Gatherings were a place to engage in dialogue, usually about the vision and direction of the union. Since the erosion of that camaraderie, the union had become nothing but a sounding board for complaints. For me, these retreats both harkened back to the old days and made me excited about the future.

• • •

The investments and properties, though critical, were largely a means to an end; they made the overhaul both possible and visually appealing. Had I stopped there, the members and perhaps even the International would have been impressed. They would have sung my praises as they made their plans for a weekend at the Kauai house or heard how much money was in our account. But unless more substantive changes were made, they would eventually see that it was all just window-dressing. Labor leaders were famous for big plans and grand gestures, but those plans were usually smoke and mirrors, a strategy to sweep the real issues under the bus.

I had always believed that in order to achieve anything, one must be willing to evaluate themselves from the perspective that they are not perfect. Every person and entity must rebrand and reeducate themselves if they hope to survive in a changing world. Those at the

International had been unwilling to do this; they just kept doing the same things over and over again and wondering why the membership continued to shrink. The stagnancy had trickled down to most locals; it was not going to happen to Local 1260.

My plan was to reinvent the union into something attractive to younger workers, who appreciated job security but wanted to be recognized on the merits of their work, not given raises and promotions purely based on seniority. To do this, they had to feel inspired and believe they made a valuable contribution to their employer.

Labor would no longer be about pounding the table, but partnering with employers so that everyone profited. Oftentimes I felt my sole job was to teach management and members to talk to each other, without the need of a third party, and if they didn't need the union—or me—anymore, I was fine with it.

Advising the youngest members had become one of the most important aspects of my job—not to mention one of my favorites. They were the future of America, and the behaviors they learned now would shape their careers for years to come. They were also the last hope for labor; more and more states were enacting right-to-work laws, and unless unions had something to offer the younger generations, they would surely face extinction.

I would routinely visit Hawaiian Electric to speak to the new hires. They were "kids" really, about twenty-two or twenty years old and just starting out in life. For most of them, college was not an option—either because they couldn't afford it or were not cut out for it—and this apprenticeship would be their ticket to home ownership, healthcare, education for their kids . . . the American dream.

"After your apprenticeship you guys will still be young, under thirty, right? With your straight time alone you'll be making $104,000 a year. Add to that your overtime and double time due to storms, cars hitting power lines, houses burning down, and Sunday shifts, and you'll be making closer to $150,000 to $200,000."

These provisions, which had been put into the contract long ago, were not only a financial incentive for workers, but a financial deterrent for employers. If they had to pay people so much money, they might be less inclined to overwork them. The union had negotiated for work-life balance, so members would have time to spend with their families. Though I'd always been a workaholic, I'd been fortunate enough to spend time with Marilyn and the kids while they were growing up, and I wanted the same for these young men.

"Put money away," I told them. "Live on your straight time, and invest the rest."

This was the point where the older guys nodded and the younger ones rolled their eyes. "Look," I said, "some of you just came from working at Kmart, making thirteen bucks an hour. You'll still be ahead of the game. You think the gravy train will last forever, but the evolution of the utility industry is here—geothermal energy, solar cars, battery packs in the car that collect the solar energy while it's sitting in the parking lot and stores it, so when you go home you can plug the car into a wall and it lights up your house. One day these technologies will be commonplace, and we won't need oil-burning plants anymore. Then what?"

"They will always need lineman," they replied. It was the arrogance of youth. They were on the rise, and I was the "dinosaur" giving them a lecture.

If I had learned anything from my experience in DC, it was that no one is expendable. But since these guys could probably not relate to that, I took a different tack.

"Everything changes. When I was your age it was inconceivable that I would be buying water from a store rather than getting it from the tap, or that I would carry a device that would allow me to make phone calls, take photos, and access information on virtually every subject known to man. Yet here I am."

This analogy earned me some more eye rolls, so I used an example closer to home. "Right now it seems we will always need linemen. But companies are in the process of creating roofing material that captures the sun. I am not talking about solar panels that are costly and must be attached, but material that inherently has this capability. Now what about if companies were to use this material on new construction throughout the country? Power lines could become a thing of the past. If you have not learned new skills, what will you do then?" This gave them pause. "We cannot stop change," I added. "We can only be responsible in the way we manage it."

Oftentimes I left these talks not quite sure whether I had gotten through to them. Many of the principles I spoke of I'd learned from my father, and I liked to think that in some small way I was preserving his legacy and perhaps even continuing the passion, purpose, and camaraderie that was once part and parcel of labor.

• • •

Trying to convince my staff of my vision was much more frustrating. As much as I tried to build a cohesive team, I often felt like I was dealing with two completely groups of people—one who was deeply committed to the work and another whose sole goal was to do as little as possible. For them, it was all about collecting a paycheck. It reminded me of something I'd read about the differences between those who were successful and those who were not. Successful people tended to feel they had a calling and a belief in something bigger than themselves. Unsuccessful people tended to whine about what was in it for them. I'd always found it curious that the people who did the least amount of work were always most concerned with when they were getting the next raise or promotion.

I always tried to inspire staff to believe in themselves and the work they were doing. "We're all here for a reason, and if we strive to uplift and empower others, we can find our place in the world," I'd tell them. "The key is to believe in something so bad it hurts inside—not just at work, but at home and in all aspects of life." At staff meetings I talked about how we were there to serve others—not just the members, but the companies that employed them, for without them everyone would starve. We were also, by extension, serving the state of Hawaii and the United States. Most of all, though, we were serving God. "God wants us to do the right thing," I told them, "which unfortunately is not necessarily the popular thing. Eventually, the truth comes out."

Though they seemed receptive to the idea, I was never sure which of the nodding heads were sincere. Of everyone in the office, Russell Takemoto would prove to be the most problematic. Throughout my first year in office, I had done everything I could to help him perform his duties as a rep, but to no avail. The problems began shortly after hiring him when I learned that he no longer had security clearance to get on the grounds of Hawaiian Electric.

Like most people, Russell had his demons, and when he was sober he hid them well enough. Unfortunately, Russell preferred to drink, and give his demons free rein. He would go from rather mild-mannered, even low energy, to a man filled with anger. His longtime girlfriend, Melanie Salvador, was the regular recipient of his aggression. On one occasion, back when he was still working for the utility company, he had spent a few nights in jail after breaking her leg. She later took him back, but Hawaiian Electric was not as forgiving. When he reapplied for security clearance as an employee of Local 1260, they denied him.

Shortly after taking office, I found myself reaching out to a company to ask for a favor on behalf of a criminal staff member, and it didn't make me feel better that they made an exception based on my relationship with them. In the end, it didn't matter; Russell accomplished nothing. I sent him to different companies, but everywhere he went, disaster followed.

One day, I arrived on Kauai for a meeting at the Pacific Missile Range Facility (PMRF), a U.S. naval base and the largest missile training and testing facility in the world. Over the years PMRF had done everything from developing the Theater Ballistic Missile Defense system capable of destroying SCUD missiles to monitoring missile launches in North Korea. Our arrangement with the facility was similar to the one in Guam; in addition to the navy people, there were civilian workers of all stripes—from plumbers to tech people to security working on the base, many of them employed by Exelis, an aerospace company and subcontractor. Local 1260 had represented them ever since 1970, when a group of workers went out on strike in order to force recognition of the union.

I had, with some trepidation, assigned the facility to Russell. Though the task was beyond him, I was far too busy to give the members the day-to-day attention they deserved, and I figured sending him would be better than nothing. Apparently, the members felt differently.

The yelling was so loud that I heard it even before I walked into the room. Russell was surrounded by a group of people; they were Local 1260 members screaming about all the things he was supposed to do for them and didn't. It had always irked me that Russell didn't answer his phone, and now I knew why.

As I walked over to see what was going on, I heard a familiar voice say, "This is not how it works, Russell. You don't understand the Service Contract Act."

The voice belonged to David Finn, a union member and part of the negotiating team at the Pacific Missile Range. The law he was referring to was the McNamara-O'Hara Service Contract Act of 1965; basically, it regulated the wages of general contractors and subcontractors working to fulfill prime contracts over $2,500. Knowledge of this law was essential to our work, and though David wasn't yelling at Russell as the others were, he did sound extremely frustrated.

Russell just stood there looking like a deer caught in the headlights. Later, he would come to resent my involvement, but for the moment he was glad I was there to step in.

After the PMRF debacle, I moved him to Hawaiian Electric Light Company on the Big Island, followed by Servco Pacific. Each time, any goodwill the union had at the company soon devolved into a screaming match. Under Russell's neglect, matters that began as trivial and easily taken care of grew to be real problems for the members.

Eventually I had to accept the fact that Russell was never going to make it as a representative. Still, part of me believed he had something to contribute, but what? Finally, I made him my chief of staff—it was an important role, but one that had little contact with members and would keep him from ruining our relationships with them.

Chapter 20

One of the strangest and most disturbing experiences during my time as business manager was the murder-for-hire accusation leveled against me by Tommy Decano. Since joining my staff, Tommy had divided his time primarily between palling around with Teresa and yelling at the ever-growing list of people who pissed him off. Performing the actual duties of his job came in a distant third.

In 2012, I decided to hold a charity golf tournament in Guam, the proceeds of which would go to Shriner's Children's Hospital and a local organization dedicating to fighting hunger. Golf had been a mainstay for Local 1260 ever since my father retired. Dad was never a fan of the sport, but I saw it as a rich fund-raising opportunity. In 1997, I started an annual tournament to raise money for education for members and their families. The first year after taking office I assigned the management of the tournament to Russell Takemoto, and like everything else I assigned him, nothing got done. With the day of the tournament rapidly approaching, I called a meeting and put Marilyn in charge. She handled tournaments from then on, and they went off without a hitch.

Despite Tommy's work history over that past year, I asked him to handle the Guam golf tournament. Ken had enough on his plate, and besides, how hard could it be? He could arrange most of it from Hawaii, then go down there and recruit people to play eighteen holes. Tommy assured me it would go off without a hitch, and for the next few months I believed him. I oversaw the project in the same manner I did everything: with a light touch and faith that my employee would rise to the occasion. All I asked was that he keep me apprised of how things were coming along.

Tom indeed gave me regular updates throughout the planning process. "It's all good, boss," he'd say. "I met with so and so." "The golf course is covered." "I'm talking to this company or that company for sponsorships." "We got 144 players signed up, and the money's coming in."

I was elated. To some, the tournament may have seemed like an insignificant event, but I saw it differently. It represented the fulfillment of my promise to Pastor Ronocco, and the others in Guam, that they would no longer be neglected by the IBEW.

When I flew down to Guam ahead of the tournament, I was shocked to find that it was not set up at all. I had no idea where Tommy got his math, but only six players had signed up, and virtually no donations had come in. I couldn't even cancel, because in reliance on Tommy's tall tales I had already pledged monies to the charities.

There I was, the former director of organizing of the entire IBEW and the present business manager of Local 1260, running around parking lots of local businesses like a chicken without a head, trying to sign people up. I wouldn't even have minded if only Tommy had been honest with me. When all was said and done, I signed up twenty players to play in the tournament. I also purchased food for the "banquet" afterward with my own money. Thank God we had some money in the charity account back in Hawaii. The event went off without a hitch, and I presented each organization with a thousand-dollar check.

After a year of dealing with Tommy, this was the final straw. When I told him he had to go, he was uncharacteristically calm. "I know I am not able to do the job the way you need me to, boss. All I ask is that you don't fight my unemployment."

Clearly, he had seen this coming, and knew there was little he could do about it. All Local 1260 staffers were "at-will," meaning I could release them at any time for any reason. It was an ironic twist, considering we worked for a labor union in a non-right-to-work state, but one I viewed as a valuable tool. In this case it was also irrelevant, because I had plenty of cause to release Tommy.

Finally, I nodded. "Don't worry about it, Tommy. You'll get your unemployment."

"Thanks, boss," he replied, and again I was taken aback by how well he was handling this.

I was even more surprised by Teresa's reaction. A few days later, she came into my office and announced she was quitting, apparently because of the way I had "treated" Tommy. For the life of me, I could not understand how this warranted her walking away from her own career. It wasn't as if she had known Tommy for all that long or was a lifer in the union. It made no sense. She opened her own legal practice, and when I went to her office to check on her and clear the air, she refused to speak with me.

About three months later, I walked out of my office and was ambushed by a flock of reporters. "Mr. Ahakuelo, is it true that you attempted to hire a former employee to commit murder?"

I felt my jaw go slack. *What?*

A second reporter was even bolder. "Brian, is Mr. Decano the only person you approached about killing your former opponent?"

Former opponent? Suddenly it dawned on me that they were talking about Lance!

I looked at them and said, "Seriously guys. This job is not that important."

At that moment, I fully expected some Hollywood type to jump out from behind a palm tree and announce that I was being punked. Unfortunately, that was not the case. Tommy was on the news, too; he had cleaned himself up, wore a sports coat, button-down shirt, and had a big, fat stogie clenched between his lips. Tommy indeed claimed that I fired him after he turned down my offer to pay him for killing Lance. He had even reported it to the cops. Aside from the obvious lunacy, I wondered what motive he would have attributed to me. Why would I want to kill someone I had already defeated? Did he think I wanted to prevent Lance from running again? I thought back to Harold's suggestion that I ruin Lance's reputation and realized that although nowhere as extreme, destroying a reputation was based on the same logic: why engage in healthy competition when you could simply destroy your opponent? The accusation also made great fodder for the local media. Just to be on the safe side, I went down to the Honolulu police station and asked to speak to the cops. An hour later, we were all laughing about it, then I went home to tell Marilyn I wasn't going to be thrown in the slammer. Marilyn didn't find the situation funny, though, especially the part where I had talked to the cops without my attorney present.

When that plan backfired, Tommy decided he would try to cash in. He filed a lawsuit against the IBEW for $700,000, which was funny because Local 1260 didn't even have that kind of money at the time. Unbelievably, he still wanted to be a union member (and pay dues!), but I reminded him that he was barred because he did not work in one of our jurisdictions.

For the next year, I sat for depositions and relived Tommy's employment so many times I think I talked about it in my sleep. Still, I refused to settle, even when the judge pointed out that, ridiculous or not, Tommy's lawyer could tie me up in court for years and at God knows what cost. I was determined to let this thing ride through the 2014 election, and when I won a second term as business manager, it would show Tommy, the media, and anyone else perpetuating the lie that the members had not been fooled.

• • •

Despite what Teresa thought, firing Tommy was not a decision I made lightly. Shortly after that golf tournament in Guam, I spent a week in Washington, DC, for the Construction Conference of the IBEW, and I took that time to mull over Tommy's performance—or lack thereof—to date. Unfortunately, while in DC, I found myself plagued by another situation that would drag on for the rest of my term.

I stayed in Crystal City, an urban area right over the bridge in Arlington, Virginia. It felt odd to be back in the nation's capital; once seen as the pinnacle of success, it had become for me the scene of deep frustration and disillusionment. Still, the experience was not unpleasant. Even in March, the city was lovely, and it was nice to be able to enjoy it, knowing I would soon be headed back to Hawaii, rather than Ed Hill's office.

Toward the end of my trip, Harold called to see if I would meet him for breakfast. He was in town attending the Building Trades Conference, an annual meeting attended by all the unions. My conference had ended the day before, so early the next morning I headed to the city, completely unaware that I was about to be railroaded.

We met at the "Hinckley Hilton," so nicknamed because it was the place where John Hinckley Jr. had tried to assassinate President Reagan in 1981. When I got there, I found Harold sitting at the table with a twentyish young man.

"This is my son, Masa," Harold said as I took my seat. "He wants to work at Hawaiian Electric."

It wasn't the first time Harold had asked me to help Masa get work. In the past he had mentioned my hiring him at Local 1260, an idea I had quickly shot down. Although I had known Masa as a boy, I hadn't seen him for many years. I had no idea about his skills, nor whether he had a strong work ethic. I could only hope it was stronger than his father's. Either way, I wasn't going to bring him on board; my staff was green enough as it was. I explained at that time that he was young—just out of high school—and that he needed to build up his experience and his maturity, just as my son had done.

"I have no influence over the hiring at Hawaiian Electric," I began, noting the annoyed look on Harold's face, "but I can try to get him into Pacific Range facility."

Harold was unimpressed. "Oh no, that's too far."

Too far? It was on the same island!

I turned to Masa. "Okay, well, there is a possibility of getting you into Osmose."

Osmose, which did business in Hawaii under the name Ikaika, was a subcontractor hired by the various utility companies, Hawaiian Electric among them, to dig holes and plant poles before linemen came in to do the electrical work. They provided a critical service and, in my opinion, were an excellent stepping-stone for someone just starting his career. Masa would have an opportunity to see whether he liked the work; he would also gain experience and some prerequisites, including his commercial driver's license, which would greatly increase his chances of being hired by a utility company later on. It was, in my opinion, almost as good as starting out at Hawaiian Electric.

"Ikaika is looking for people," I added, "but I will tell you right now, Masa, it's hard work."

Harold nodded dismissively. "Just see about Hawaiian Electric, will you?"

By that time, I wanted to remind Harold that he was supposed to be in a meeting. Instead, he lingered over the meal long enough to needle me about Hawaiian Electric. When the bill arrived, he let me pay it without argument, though he had a per diem meal allowance for which he did not have to hand in receipts.

When I got back to Hawaii, I made a few calls on Masa's behalf. The first confirmed what I already knew—I could not get him into Hawaiian Electric. One of the vice presidents at Ikaika, however, was more receptive.

"We work well with you, Brian," he said, which only made me feel more uncomfortable about asking for a favor. "Have the kid come down and fill out an application."

Shortly afterward, Masa was indeed hired by Ikaika, and I thought I was free of Harold's nagging. I wasn't. Hardly a day went by that he didn't complain that his son was making seventeen dollars an hour, rather than twenty.

"He's only eighteen years old," I pointed out. "He's not going to go from A to Z within a few months. Besides, doesn't he want to go to college?"

"No, he just wants to get in at Hawaiian Electric."

About two weeks later, I received word that Masa had not been showing up to work. I was too busy—not to mention aggravated—to deal with it myself, but I could not ignore the issue, either. I asked Brandon, who served as Ikaika's rep, to check it out.

The situation was what I had been afraid of. The vice president had hesitated to call me because it was awkward. I was livid, mostly at myself for jeopardizing a good relationship for a kid I hardly knew. Not that I'd had much choice; Harold would not have given me a minute's peace if I refused.

"You need to get in touch with Masa," I told Harold. "He has an attendance problem."

"This is not my job; it is yours," Harold snapped, then added, "He better stay employed."

It was one of the few times in my life when I've been speechless. Not that it was all that surprising; passing the buck was Harold's specialty. Apparently, he thought it was my responsibility, not only to rein Masa in but to prevent the company from firing him.

"What's going on, Masa?" I said when I finally tracked him down. "You know I put myself out there for you."

"But, Uncle, I'm tired in the morning," he whined. "I see I'm going to be fifteen minutes late, so I just stay out the whole day."

I don't know what was more infuriating—his lame excuse or his use of the endearment uncle, which in Hawaiian was a sign of respect for an unrelated elder. But that wasn't even the worst of it. He had apparently gone around the company bragging that the union had gotten him the job. He even used my name.

"You better get yourself to work," I told him, though I had the sneaking suspicion this would do no good. He was not only immature, but lazy, and it was being encouraged by his father.

"Masa needs more money," he told me one day. "His girlfriend is pregnant." With these words he launched another campaign designed to get me to get him a job at Hawaiian Electric.

"If he goes to work," I quipped, "he'll make more money."

Harold ignored the comment. "You know, Masa's girlfriend lives on Kauai, so it would be easier if he worked there. What about KIUC?"

I almost laughed in his face at that one.

Shortly before I left DC, bidding had started on a solar project on Kauai; it was going to be the largest commercial solar farm in the state. When the labor community learned that Solar City, a nonunion company, had gotten the contract, they were livid, and no one more so than Harold Dias. Never mind that once again unions, with their exorbitant wage demands, had succeeded only in pricing themselves out of the market. Now, in the twenty-third hour, Harold called me, demanding that I fight them on it.

"What does this have to do with me?" I felt like I was always asking Harold that question.

"Well, they are a utility company, so it has everything to do with you."

"But when did this job come up? When was it bid on?"

He shrugged. "A few years ago."

"Exactly."

For the life of me I would never understand Harold's motivations, specifically why he wanted to recruit me to every manipulative scheme he thought up. Solar panels were considered construction and therefore clearly under the jurisdiction, not of Local 1260, but of Local 1186, which was run by Harold's close friend Damien Kim.

When I pointed this out to him, Harold waved dismissively. "Well, if you won't do it, Damien and I will go straight to David Bissell."

There was a time when I would have cautioned Harold against doing this, but I knew he wouldn't listen. *This thing is going to crash and burn.* David Bissell was the president of KIUC, and a heck of a nice guy, but he was no pushover.

Sure enough, Harold and Damien barged into Bissell's office and demanded that the project go union. I could only imagine what happened next—Bissell explained that the company would have to break contracts—and in all likelihood be sued—and all so they could pay union workers eighty bucks an hour, which was double what they were paying Solar City. As Harold and Damien had little regard for the facts, they probably ranted until Bissell asked them to leave or his assistant came in and made up an excuse about a phone call or a meeting.

The matter was far from over, though. The co-op was not structured like a regular utility company. The "people" owned it, and held an election every few years to vote on the executive board. After the solar project went nonunion, Harold decided to throw his hat in the ring. On the night of the election, I called him up to see how he was doing.

"They're going to pick the top three for positions," Harold says. "I'm trying to figure out whether I am going to be first, second, or third."

It was good to have confidence, but I had a feeling Harold's was misplaced. I called Tracy Acinto, a Local 1260 board member from Kauai, and asked whether she had heard anything. The news was not good.

"Harold's burnt all his bridges on Kauai," Tracy said.

Sure enough, at last count, Harold had come in a dismal eighth place. When he got the news, he once again laid the blame at my feet.

"If you worked harder," he said, "I would have won."

Now he had the gall to ask me to pull strings for Masa at KIUC.

This annoyed me to no end. David and I had a good relationship, but things could go south rather quickly if I vouched for Masa and he didn't show up to work. As I picked up the phone to call David, I told myself I wasn't doing this for Harold, but for his unborn grandchild. We made the unusual niceties, then I made a soft pitch. As always, David was courteous but clear: he had no control over who got hired. Masa didn't get the job, and Harold continued to pressure me to find something for him.

Eventually, I got Masa a job with a subcontractor on Oahu. After sitting him down for a talk about work ethic, I said, "The job is on Oahu, but it pays twenty dollars an hour plus overtime. Your baby will be better off if you're on another island and working than sitting on your butt on Kauai. And your girlfriend will definitely like you more."

Chapter 21

The primary role of the chief of staff was to handle the day-to-day operations of the office, and more importantly, to set an example for the rest of the staff. As business manager, my primary function was to protect the jurisdictions of Local 1260, and to do this I had to be visible in the community. When I wasn't meeting with politicians and CEOs, I attended board meetings or consulted with financial people about our financial investments. That left Russell to supervise the rest of the staff and make sure they were meeting the needs of the members. Unfortunately, Russell was singularly uninterested in doing so.

Just as I had done the first year, I continued to coach him around his job skills, not to mention his personal issues. It did little good. Takemoto was constantly out on sick leave. For the most part, he blamed it on his big toe, or more accurately the gout that inflamed it. Gout, a type of arthritis caused by an excess of uric acid in the body, was excruciating and could affect virtually any area of the body, though it most commonly settled in the toe. It was also exacerbated by alcohol, which was the root cause of all Russell's problems.

He'd get drunk after work and try to intimidate the staff, and the next morning he'd either show up hungover or not at all. Takemoto's father was a menace as well; a staunch Republican, he'd come down to the union hall to fight with the staff because we supported President Obama. Apparently, it had escaped his notice that Hawaii was not only the president's home state, but possibly the bluest in the land. I didn't have to spend much time with the elder Takemoto to understand why Russell drank. "What are you doing, Russell?" I'd say to him after he'd gone on yet another bender. "If you don't knock off the vodka, you're going to kill yourself."

I'd get some mumbled excuse in response, sometimes a half-hearted agreement to try, then things would continue as usual. Sometimes I felt like my real job was hunting him down so I could find out when I could expect this or that task to be completed.

"Answer my calls and texts," I'd tell him. "For God's sake, people are waiting for their expenses to be processed."

The executive board met in our offices on the first Friday of each month. I would report on what the reps had done for the month, from the meetings they attended to which employee had been accused of what infraction. Usually I had to present roughly eighteen matters, not including the financial reports, which were done by Russell's girlfriend, Melanie Salvador. I had brought her on board in 2013 to handle the accounting, as by that time Marilyn was up to her neck in community outreach projects.

Ahead of each board meeting, I would remind Russell about the reports. "Make sure they come in by Tuesday so Leeann can put them all together and I can review them on Thursday."

"Sure, Boss," Russell would say, and each month I would tell myself that this time he would come through.

Then Friday would roll around, and Leeann would to come up to me and say, "The board meeting's in a few hours and we still don't have reports from all the reps."

I'd ask her why, even though I knew the answer.

Leeann would shrug, but the answer was clear. Then, instead of preparing for the meeting, I'd find myself managing Russell.

"Oh, there is a board meeting today?" he'd ask, as if he had been working there for two weeks instead of two years.

"Well, yes Russell, there is, just as there is the first Friday of every month."

"Oh, jeez," he'd say sheepishly, "I forgot to send out the email."

Finally, I told Leeann to collect the reports herself. When she went ahead and did so, Russell had the nerve to become indignant.

"That's my job."

"Why aren't you doing it then?"

He'd grumble, "I got a lot of stuff I have to do," and when I questioned him about it, he'd rattle off a list of medical excuses.

Oftentimes, he didn't show up at all, and I'd be forced to stop whatever I was doing and go look for him. When I'd gather with the others, I was met with blank looks and a surprised-sounding, "Oh, he didn't come to work today?"

Though they couldn't stand Russell, they hated the thought of causing tension even more. They would tell me not to get upset, but how could I not be? Russell had turned me into the type of boss I loathed—the one watching the clock and walking into offices to keep tabs on people. Only when everyone else denied seeing him did I head down the hall to Melanie's office. I absolutely dreaded speaking with her about it.

"Hey Mel, is Russ around?"

"Don't know."

"Well, did he come to work?"

"Don't know."

This attitude made my blood boil. She had lived with the man for twenty years, and they usually came into work together. Sometimes I'd look outside and see Russell's union car sitting outside! Melanie had left him hungover, clutching his toe, or both, and driven it to work. Still, she had no problem lying to my face.

Seeing he could not handle his duties, I moved him around and gave him other stuff, but he allowed his personal issues and resentments to prevent him from accomplishing anything. Worse yet, the rest of the staff despised him, complaining about him constantly. No one liked him less than Michael Brittain.

• • •

Tommy's and Teresa's abrupt departures left me with two significant holes in my staff that had to be filled immediately. Michael Brittain was in his forties—young for the labor world—and worked at the Hawaiian Electric plant. I did not know him all that well, other than he was interested enough in the union to attend membership meetings. During the interview he said he believed he was qualified because he'd been in the army, and though his duties at Local 1260 would be quite unrelated to military service, I didn't need an excuse to give a veteran a chance. Besides, I told myself, how much worse than Tommy could he be?

I would soon have my answer, and the answer was, *a lot worse.* Brittain could not get the simplest tasks done. He constantly called in sick, and on the days he did show up, he refused to stay more than a couple of hours. Sometimes he told me he was not feeling well; other times he just announced he could not work past noon, as if no further explanation was needed. He was seemingly competing with Russell Takemoto for worst job performance.

"You gotta get out there and meet with the members," I'd tell him. "Go over any issues they have . . ."

His responses to this ranged from, "I am not going to work with that guy" to an equally lame, "I got a headache."

I'd find out later that he'd spent the afternoon coaching a soccer game.

When he was in the office he spent most of his time on his hob-by-slash-side business, graphic design. Most people would have the decency to be startled when their boss caught them drawing on their computer time and time again, but not Brittain. Sometimes it took every ounce of strength to keep my cool.

"The members are paying us, Michael. Not working is like stealing from members."

To this he'd respond with an incredulous stare. I was dealing with a child in a man's body.

He was not much different socially. The rest of the staff told me he was a jerk and that they could not work with him. Even his wife was not immune; he often yelled at her in front of others, which was embarrassing for everyone present. Even his greatest credential turned out to be a lie. One day the subject of Brittain's military service came up.

As time went on, I learned that he also had a history of acting against the interests of his fellow members. When Lance called his infamous strike during the storm of 2011, Brittain had stood on the sidelines, selling T-shirts, then bragged about the thousands of dollars he had made off the members. Before coming to Hawaii he had been a mechanic at United Airlines' Indianapolis hub. When the company hit hard times, they presented workers with a choice—they could agree to a small, temporary reduction in pay, or the hub would have to close. Though the reduction was minimal—just twenty-five cents an hour—Brittain went around lobbying everyone to vote no. "Screw the company," he said. He must have been convincing, though, because the members voted down the measure. Sure enough, the hub shut down. Had Brittain cared about his "brothers," he could have suggested building a time limit into the agreement, requesting retroactive pay when the crisis was over, or something else to sweeten the pot. Instead, he took pleasure in sticking it to company. The fact that he bragged about it, even after he and everyone else lost their jobs, was a testament to his enormous ego and shortsightedness. That the others had agreed with him was indicative of a larger, more pervasive problem in labor, but for the time being I had to focus on what was going on in my own backyard. How was I to carve out another way forward with people like Brittain on my staff?

The only thing worse than dealing with Brittain was dealing with Brittain and Takemoto together. The two shared an instant animosity, based on each man's need to control and dominate everyone and everything around them. Once, while in Boston for a meeting, they nearly came to blows. The argument began in the hotel bar and continued to escalate once we got to the room. Only after I threatened them with termination did they retreat to their respective corners before blood was shed.

• • •

I also had to hire a rep to replace Teresa, preferably another attorney so I could continue saving on legal fees. Enter Amy Ejercito, an attorney and former vice president at Hawaiian Election. She had lost her job with them back in 2007 when a new administration took over, saying only that she wasn't a "good fit." I knew enough about office politics not to be dissuaded by that. It could have been a simple matter of the new management bringing in their own people. Since then she had been working in the HR department at the Hilton, Hawaii Village. That choice would turn out to be the source of more than one headache in the coming years, not just for me, but to those sitting across the negotiating table from her.

From the beginning, Amy clearly had her quirks. When she travelled, she booked two rooms, one for herself and another for her voluminous files, with no regard for the cost to the members. She often shuffled into work around ten or eleven each morning, even when she had things to do around the office and no matter how many times I spoke to her about it. She did show up to eight a.m. staff meetings, but she complained about it every time. "Can't you make them later, Brian?" she'd whine. "I always have to get up so early."

One thing I was strict about was that people were on time to meetings. I had always shown my superiors—including Ed Hill and others I did not see eye to eye with—the respect of showing up to their meetings on time. If I scheduled a staff meeting at eight a.m., I expected them to be in the conference room at eight, not just rolling out of bed or shuffling around the office with a coffee cup.

Some, like Leeann and Jennifer, appreciated the freedom of environment while understanding that they still had to adhere to professional standards. When I told them to dress how they felt comfortable and most creative, they knew this did not mean wearing shorts and flip-flops when they accompanied me to meetings of the Salary Commission for the City Council of Honolulu or the Labor Relations Board for the IRRA. It was imperative that decision makers from various companies saw us as equals when they determined who would receive a scholarship or how much they would contribute to a charity golf tournament.

Michael Brittain and Amy were of a completely different mindset. They felt entitled to have and do what they wanted.

"It's not the color I want," Michael Brittain said of the car I leased for his use. "And couldn't you have gotten the sports package?"

I nearly bit my tongue in half trying to hold back a retort. "This is for business, to go from point A to point B; that's it."

"Well, I just won't use it."

Amy was the same way. Many mornings I found myself sitting alone in the office before the others got in, knowing that just like the International, my staff had lost their way. They had forgotten what being in the union was about; perhaps they had never known at all. Maybe I had simply made it too easy for them. Whatever the case, we were certainly not all on the same page. Bringing a vision to fruition didn't concern them, as this required focusing on the work in front of them. All they cared about was the future—what was in it for them and how quickly it would arrive. It was a ripe environment for rumors, and they looked to me for clarification.

More than once a staff member told me that Michael Brittain was going around claiming he would be the next business manager.

"Last time I looked," I replied in disgust, "I was still the business manager, and I'm not going anywhere. Why don't you just be happy where you are?"

Chapter 22

Time and again I brought someone on board, believing that even if they lacked experience for the position, they had the heart for it. For me, what someone had done in the past was not important, what mattered was their commitment to something bigger than themselves. As time went on and I was disappointed by yet another staff member, I began to question my own judgment.

At first Russell Yamanoha and I seemed to be on the same page. I had created the position of communications director to remind the public that union members were not devils who intentionally made them suffer during a storm, but their neighbors and friends who coached baseball teams and contributed to charities. As a veteran of local media, Yamanoha seemed a perfect fit.

Since Yamanoha was from Maui, I also charged him with repping the three hundred members working at Maui Electric, with the eventual goal of making him that island's Outer Island rep. As with so many other aspirations I had for my staff, this goal turned out to be a pipe dream. Every time an issue came up, it would turn into a fiasco. Russell Yamanoha would listen to the members and management, but he never made a decision.

Finally, I told him, "Don't go, I'll talk to them." It was like Takemoto all over again.

When I got to Maui Electric, I once again found myself facing a mob of angry members. Now, I always backed up my staff, so long as they made professional, educated decisions in a caring way. But this was not a case of members complaining just to complain; their needs were being ignored. "Let me know what's going on," I said, "so I can fix it."

It would have been well within my rights to fire Yamanoha, but I refused to consider this option, partly out of loyalty. Hawaii was an insular and tight-knit community, and I had known most of the people I was dealing with for my entire life. It was not easy to thrust them out into the street, much as I would have liked to. Another part of me—a part I hated to acknowledge—was still shaken from the Tommy Decano business. If he could accuse me of attempting to hire a hit man, what would the next person do?

Since I could not have Russell further alienating Maui Electric either, I moved him over to the broadcasting side. At that time Local 1260 serviced all the TV stations in Hawaii, and I figured for Russell it would be like coming home.

For a while, it seemed I had made the right decision. Russell regularly reported that he had visited this station or that, spoke to the members, and that everything was going fine. No one said anything to the contrary, so it didn't even occur to me to check up on him. Then one day, while at a meeting in California, I got a call from Hawaii

News Now. They were letting me know they had filed a petition with the regional NLRB office to decertify the union.

My mouth literally dropped. What could have happened to make them want to decertify? If there was a problem, surely Russell would have let me know.

When I met with the employees, I was shocked to learn that they had not seen Russell in a year! Hawaii News Now was a news department used jointly by three different local television stations: the NBC, CBS, and MyNetworkTV affiliates, and employees from each were tired of paying dues and getting nothing in return. And Russell's accounts of smooth sailing at the stations? All fabrications. It was difficult to listen after that, because all I could think about was how yet another person I'd trusted had made me look like a complete fool.

I did whatever I could to keep the members from voting to decertify. Normally, they would have been precluded from doing so because we had a contract, but Hawaii News Now had a window in their agreement. I had never worried about it before, because I knew I would never have allowed the relationship to deteriorate to that point. It never occurred to me that someone in my employ would lie to my face on a regular basis. I had time to be furious about that later; right now I had to deal with the situation in front of me. I tried to smooth things over with the members, but they did not want to hear anything I had to say. They were well within their rights to dump us, and they had made up their mind. The only thing I could do was let them de-authorize, then work to rebuild the relationship. For a minimal dues fee of fifty dollars, I would let them apply for union jobs as freelance journalists and photogs. That appeased them somewhat, and I left angry, drained, yet hopeful that they would at some point choose to rejoin the union.

Until that day I usually faulted the business manager when the member roster plummeted. Now, for the first time I understood the damage incompetent staff could do. Since I wasn't willing to clean house, I had to figure something else out before we had no more members to rep.

• • •

Later, claims would be made by the union—and by extension, the media—that I had hired my family members for personal gain. In part, it was just an attempt on the part of the union to ruin my name. There was nothing in the bylaws that prohibited hiring family; indeed, if they had a problem with so-called "nepotism," they would have balked when my father hired me in the early 90s! The fact was, labor was often a family business, passed down from generation to generation, and that included several of my accusers.

Even beyond the slander, though, was a fundamental misunderstanding on the part of the IBEW as to why I brought my family on board. When one has a fundamental belief in something, whether it is a religious faith or a political or social cause, it literally becomes the fabric of who they are. For me, my commitment to labor and my spiritual beliefs were intertwined. It was about being of service to others, feeling gratitude for what God had blessed me with, and trying to be a force for good in the world. This was not my own doing—it had been passed down to me from my parents, from the schools they sent me to and the way they taught me to treat people, to the camaraderie I witnessed at the union and the actual gains my father brought to the members. I in turn had passed their values down to my children. Eventually, I would realize that labor was not the only way to achieve my larger goal; it was simply the vehicle I had been given. I suppose in that regard I should thank those who betrayed me on May 6, 2016, for they made it impossible for me to continue trying to create a sustainable model for unions moving forward. My decision to hire those closest to me was not just ideological, but practical. There was no way I could keep Local 1260 going with the staff I had, and I knew my family members would work as hard as I did to get the job done.

Marilyn had been on the Local 1260 staff from the beginning. Initially, I brought her on board to help with the clerical duties, but the eventual goal was for her to head up the community outreach program. With her mix of media, education, and administrative experience—as well as her connections in the community—I could not have asked for a better candidate.

Marilyn's sister, Jennifer Estencion, also proved to be an invaluable addition to my staff. When I offered her the job in 2012, she had been working at Hawaiian Electric for fifteen years. Yet she accepted without hesitation, even though she gave up a secure position for one she could lose if I was not reelected. Just by taking the job, she showed more faith in the future of Local 1260 than most of my staff. Throughout my tenure, my commitment to Guam never wavered. As promised, I continued to go down there once a month, mostly to reassure the members that they had not been forgotten.

I also took over Tommy Decano's role regarding Guam. Though Ken cared about his job and had continued to develop his skills, he still needed oversight. I left him responsible for the day-to-day servicing of the contracts, but he now reported directly to me regarding the needs of the members and/or companies. It added to my already significant workload, but it was better than playing referee between Ken and someone else, or even worse, finding out Ken had been the problem in the first place.

For the most part this setup worked fine. Once out from under Tommy's thumb, Ken continued to build his relationships down there; however, it was nearly impossible to do this and keep up with administrative tasks. That's where Jennifer came in.

Although her main role was to serve as one of my executive assistants, she was also charged with taking care of the Guam office. Most of the time she was able to take care of things from Hawaii, but when Ken got overwhelmed, I would ask her to go down on one of my trips and help him catch up.

After awhile I started asking her to go down there alone, usually for a week at a time. She'd spend a few days filing, making sure all the union cards were signed and whatever else he needed, then make the hellish return trip home. This worked for a while, then I got word from a Ken. He was drowning in paperwork, and it would require more than a week of assistance. When I asked Jen to go for a month, her eyes widened slightly. "I really need you to get the office up to speed."

She nodded, but I wasn't done. I figured if she didn't think I was crazy yet, she certainly would now. "The thing is, Jen, I don't want to spend that kind of money on a hotel. Would you be willing to sleep at the office?"

Her eyes got even wider, then she nodded again. The office was pretty small, but it had a shower and ample space for a futon. Jen spent the next month learning how to make ramen noodles interesting. It wasn't something she wanted to do, but she did it because she was committed to the members and didn't want to waste their money. She also knew that I didn't ask people for things I wouldn't do myself. When I went on trips to DC, I would use my own points. When money was tight, everyone took a pay cut, mine being the biggest. Anyone else in the office would have laughed in my face.

Turns out, the futon would serve another purpose. One day a former board member now serving as a local rep in Guam called, begging me to let him sleep at the office. His wife had kicked him out after learning that he was having an affair with a coworker, and now he had no money and no place to stay. I was tempted to tell him to go sleep at his girlfriend's house, but apparently that relationship had gone south as well. Finally I said yes. I didn't have the heart to make him sleep in the street, and I didn't want to put it on Ken to lend him money. He camped for three or four weeks, just long enough for him to convince his wife to take him back.

By 2013, I came to the realization that I needed to bring another representative on board. Dealing with the Russells was draining my energy and threatening the relationships with employers and members. I had a choice: I could either continue to put out fires or I could get someone in there I trusted and move forward with my plans. One person came to mind: Brandon. He was certainly qualified, having worked at Potomac Electric for ten years. As a union member, he was well aware of workers' needs and aspirations; as my son, he knew and shared my philosophies with regard to labor and life in general. He was also able to communicate with the younger generations, thereby bridging the gap that had existed in labor for decades. Most important, though, was that I trusted him completely.

I knew it was a lot to ask. Brandon and Neiani had built a good life in Virginia, and they were in no rush to uproot the kids and return to the state with the highest cost of living in the nation. They would also be leaving Megan and Eric—whom they were extremely close with—behind. Yet they came, no questions asked, and joined the rat race that was Local 1260. Brandon hit the ground running and was soon building a reputation as a liaison between members and their employers. Neiani also joined the team as one of my executive assistants. They started working at five a.m. and often didn't quit until eight at night. Thanks to them, Local 1260 took a giant step forward, something for which I would always be grateful. Unfortunately, I would also put them in the line of fire when my political enemies decided to get me out.

• • •

The business manager position is like any other; one can do the bare minimum needed to get by, or can take the job and the organization in new, expansive directions. When my father ran Local 1260, he was a recognizable figure in the community, and one seen as a force for good. Since then, stature of the local had deteriorated along with the rest of labor. I was living in different times, with different challenges and tools at my disposal, but my father remained my standard of what it meant to be a leader. Dad had always believed in leading by example, and he never demanded from others what he wouldn't do himself. I was the same way with my staff, and that included making decisions that affected my wallet right along with theirs.

Though the sale of the land was an enormous leap forward, it would not ensure the prosperity of Local 1260 forever. In fact, given the fiscal mismanagement I had witnessed throughout labor over the years, I knew that $5.4 million could be lost as easily as the $500,000 with which I had begun my term. If we wanted to protect our members and allow the coffers to grow, we needed to install new policies and procedures that would guide even the most inept hand and give us options in the event that communications between us and an employer broke down. In other words, although striking was always my last resort, I needed to know we had the resources to do it, and the companies needed to be aware of it too.

In 2013, after careful review of benefits, I decided to change the medical benefits for retired union staff. Up to that point, all retirees *and their families* received coverage—including prescriptions, at no cost, for life. Even after the former employee died, his or her spouse continued to be covered. While I understood that this was not something to be thrown away lightly, I simply could not justify the cost to members. It was the precisely the kind of thing that put the entire organization at risk down the road.

At the next board meeting, I proposed that, moving forward, only the employee would be covered after they retired. Current employees and their families would continue to be covered. Although it did not affect their medical benefits—those were managed by their particular employer—the members still had to vote on it. The proposal passed easily and became part of Local 1260's policies. Such policies were particular to each local and were safeguarded by the business manager.

I also made changes to the percentage staff members contributed to the pension, something that was in my sole discretion as business manager and did not require board approval. These were not one-time changes, but could be adjusted depending on the current financial situation. When money was tight, I reduced the amount, one time going as low as 2%. Four or five months later, when things improved, I brought it back up, one time going as high as 15%. Again, this never affected the members' pensions, which like the medical benefits were handled by employers; I would simply negotiate for certain parameters.

Finances, however, were only part of the equation. For me, no moments were more precious than connecting with members. When I

was running in 2011, one of the members' biggest complaints was that
they did not have a business manager who communicated with them.
One of the first things I did was create Facebook, Twitter, YouTube,
and other social media accounts; this gave me a way to broadcast my
plans for the union to members, and several different ways for them
to connect with me and my staff. However, this would not replace the
face-to-face contact; like any constituency, Local 1260's members
wanted a leader who took a personal interest in their lives.

We had hundreds of members who, because of their schedules,
were unable to attend membership meetings. To Marilyn's dismay, I
would often leave home in the middle of the night to walk through a
plant and talk to those on the graveyard shift, or a television station
to speak to photogs—or freelance photographers—who couldn't come
to meetings during the day. I'd bring them pastries and shoot the bull
with them, but really it was about letting the members know I was a
real person with a genuine commitment to them. I'd ask them if they
had any questions or concerns about union business, and if I couldn't
answer then might then and there, I'd promise to take them to the
next board or member meeting. In fact, attendance at membership
meetings was quite low because I dealt with issues out in the field.

Of course, some guys still complained. "I don't use Facebook,"
they'd say.

"So call me."

"Why do *I* have to call *you*?" For these guys, nothing was ever
good enough; no one had ever done enough for them. But I couldn't
truly get angry with them; their attitude had been fostered by union

leadership for decades. The only way to change them was to show them another way. So I started calling up certain guys every now and again to see if they had any issues.

"No," they'd say, genuinely surprised, "I don't, but I appreciate the call, man."

This was the personal touch that is the heart of any business, union or for-profit. It also tended to curtail grumblings about trivial things and kept members focused on issues that really mattered.

• • •

Even with my family there, I found it impossible to slow down. It seemed no matter how much we accomplished, there was always something more to be done. Marilyn would beg me to rest, but except for the rare vacation, I worked seven days a week. I'd always been somewhat of a workaholic, but this was different. When I wasn't attending to the finances or visiting with members, I sat in on contract negotiations or oversaw property renovations.

This was all secondary to inspiring the members. Each month, I would post a video on YouTube, discussing the direction of Local 1260 and its place in the community. "There is no substitute for the strength of companies in this country," I told them, "nor the resilience and determination of the American workforce."

The central message of each video, however, was not about the companies, but the members themselves. It was this appreciation of the individual that enticed the younger generations to join a union. To gauge our success, we would check the "back end" of our website to see how many people were looking at it. It even told us where they were located. Imagine my delight when I saw that people from as far away as Africa had checked it out! I also saw that people from DC were looking, and couldn't help but assume it was the International. It only added to my satisfaction, for it would have been a cold day in hell before Ed Hill would have ever let me create something like that.

"Believe in yourselves," I said on the next video, "as your strength and passion will resonate into success in everything you do in life."

• • •

While I was relatively lax with the rest of my staff, I was rather hard on my family. In addition to our regular duties, we all sat on various boards throughout the state. I was on the Industrial Relations Research Association and the Honolulu City Council Salary Commission; Brandon was a State Land Use Commission Member; and Marilyn was on the Labor Community Service Committee. They knew that unless they could not get out of bed, they better not call in sick. For this, I paid them on the low end of the scale as outlined in the bylaws. They understood the need to avoid any appearance of impropriety, as well as the need the save the members money. And when money was tight at Local 1260, my family and I were the first to take pay cuts. The way I drove them, it was a wonder they didn't hate me. Instead, they showed me nothing but support.

At times I didn't know why I pushed so hard. Partly it was the opportunity to effect real, sustainable change, but I also couldn't help feeling that if I stopped, it might all fall apart. I was determined not to let that happen, even at the cost of my own health.

Although my father had passed away from liver cancer, it had originally begun in his colon. That meant that starting at age forty, I went every three years for a colonoscopy. After a few negative tests, the doctor assured me they would extend that to every five years, but that was little comfort when I was home dealing with the prep the day before the test. It was then, between glasses of thick, chalky liquid, that a critical issue with the PUC came up. The commission was talking about not allowing Maui Electric to recover the base rate, or what they charged the customer, any longer. For example, if a customer received a one-hundred-dollar electric bill, some went toward the actual usage, while the rest went for things like labor costs, pensions, and medical insurance of the workers; in other words, the operating costs of the company. Not surprisingly, the CEO was a nervous wreck, and I found myself in the middle.

"We can't have that," I said when he mentioned the very real threat to the members' medical, dental, vision, and drug coverage. This put him slightly at ease, but my work was just beginning. The rest of my day was divided evenly between phone calls with the governor, nasty drinks, and trips to the bathroom.

The test itself was a breeze by comparison; in fact, it was the best sleep I'd had in over a year.

"Don't you dare go back to work," the hospital staff told me. "It was light anesthesia, but still, you must go home and sleep for a few hours."

To Marilyn's relief, I didn't argue with them but followed her out to the car. She dropped me off at the home we shared with Brandon and Neiani, comfortable in the knowledge that my daughter-in-law was around to look in on me. I had just sat down to rest when Harold Dias called, prattling on about some trivial construction issue. Why wasn't Damien getting work, he wanted to know. Why was Kauai Electric building a solar farm, and how come they were using non-union workers?

It was the same sort of thing he had complained about a hundred times before, but today it got under my skin.

"What does that have to do with me?" I asked, which of course was the wrong thing to say if I wanted to end the conversation.

As we argued back and forth, the strangest sensation spread over my body. Then my legs just gave way. I kneeled down by a chair but managed to keep my voice steady.

"Harold, I might have to call you back. I am busy right now."

I ended the call just as Neiani walked into the room. "Dad!" she said, clearly alarmed, "come with me right now."

She looked so stern as she led me to the couch and ordered me to lie down, I was almost afraid of her. After making sure I was comfortable and had a glass of water nearby, she left the room with my cell phone still clutched in her hand.

Chapter 23

In December of 2014, President Obama signed the Kline-Miller Multiemployer Pension Reform Act into law. Created through collective bargaining, multiemployer plans pooled a multitude of benefits for workers, including vacation and sick leave, life and unemployment insurance, and pensions for retirees. By 2014, there were 2,671 such plans in the U.S., managing $700 billion in assets.

Under the new law, which was part of the 2015 omnibus spending bill, unions whose pension funds were in danger of becoming insolvent could reduce benefits for both active workers and retirees. Approval of the reduction would be at the discretion of the Treasury Department, then the plan's trustees would determine how to apply the cuts. This meant, for example, that they could make deeper cuts in retirees' benefits than those of active workers, so long as those retirees were not age eighty or older and were not collecting disability benefits. Officially, members had to vote on the cuts, but it was a right in name only. First, a majority of the plan's participants, not just those voting, had to vote against the cuts. Second, even if this did happen, the Treasury Department could override it, if in conjunction with the Department of Labor and the Pension Benefit

Guaranty Corporation—a government insurance company that bailed out troubled pensions—decided the cuts were necessary.

While prounion organizations lobbied hard for the law, opponents called it a "sweetheart deal," a barb aimed at both the chronic fiscal mismanagement and the reputation labor leaders had for accepting bribes. It was an assessment I wholeheartedly agreed with. I also noted several troubling aspects of the law, including the fact that benefits would not automatically be restored if the union's financial outlook improved. Also, the trustees' decision could be overturned only by the Treasury Department and only if it was "clearly erroneous." Though the law did not directly affect me—I was not responsible for handling members' pensions—it made me more determined than ever to make sure that Local 1260 was not just solvent, but thriving, long after I left office.

• • •

Earlier that same year, I ran for reelection as business manager. Harold Dias, who had been both an ally and a manipulator throughout my first term, wholeheartedly supported my bid for a second. Lance had thrown his hat in the ring again, along with Sam Cadelinia, who worked at Hawaiian Electric. Unfortunately, Sam did not correctly follow the procedure to get himself on the ballot. Harold was appalled when I told him I'd offered to take Sam to another meeting to ask the members to nominate him.

"Brian, are you crazy? This is the perfect opportunity to get rid of him!"

I shrugged. "He wants to run; let him run."

Truth be told, I was not concerned about Sam. Even if I was, it wouldn't have changed my decision. In my book, winning by circumventing the democratic process was no win at all. I needed to know that the members were not voting for me by default, but were happy with my performance and the direction I was taking Local 1260. On election night, I got my answer. I won by nine hundred votes—which amounted to a ringing endorsement of what I had done over the last three years. Sam came in last, but he remained grateful that he'd been able to run.

I was further encouraged when, that same year, Harold approached me about taking my model nationwide. He wanted it to be used as the basis for workshops to be used at locals across the country.

On the other hand, Harold did not approve of many of my methods, particularly my attempts at relationship-building with the employers. When I smiled and shook hands over the negotiating table, he thought I was being obsequious; when I did not argue with management, he thought I was giving away the farm. He did not realize that I was employing tactical strategies honed after decades of dealing with different types of people. These strategies, such as building up financial equity and leverage were only possible when a foundation of trust existed between the parties; they were also highly effective. One example of this was the gentleman's agreement I had with the CEO of Hawaiian Electric. When work came in, they would look first to hire union members, so long as they had the freedom to hire non-union when it was more fiscally beneficial. When the International found out about this arrangement, they promptly said I should get the company to sign an agreement to use another local's contractors.

"But there is no need," I told them. "We have a verbal agreement that they will use IBEW contractors, and as long as I am here, they will honor that."

I explained that the company might use Local 1260, it might be 1186, which was Damien's local, but it would be IBEW. On the other hand, they would not be boxed into using union labor to their detriment. This was one of those cases when labor had shot itself in the foot. Sometimes, the work didn't bring in enough money to warrant paying union wages; other times the Public Utilities Commission would tell them they had to use the cheapest labor available. I refused to tie the company's hands; to the ego-based negotiator, such a thing would have felt like a victory, but it would have ruined any chance at an authentic relationship and hurt the membership in the long run. Harold and the boys at the International hated this idea.

For example, in a given year there might be $100 million in work to contract, over and above the work the company's in-house guys (who were all members of Local 1260 anyway) would do, such as maintaining the distribution lines that serviced the residential areas. This extra work would include all the things Hawaiian Electric employees did not do, such as planting poles, digging holes, and handling the transmission lines, which were those that were high voltage and went across the country.

Harold demanded that we get the agreement in writing, specifically demanding that they use Local 1186.

"They will never go for that," I told him. "And as I said, we have an agreement already, an agreement that includes Damien's local as well."

"That's if you're here," Harold snapped. I then realized what this was all about; my verbal pact with Hawaiian Electric gave me too much power.

• • •

Toward the end of 2014, the state of Hawaii also elected a new governor. During a contentious primary season, former state senator and Pearl City native David Ige pulled off a stunning upset, garnering 66% of the vote to defeat sitting governor and fellow Democrat Neil Abercrombie in the primary. The once-popular Abercrombie had managed to alienate several of the groups—including unions—who had gotten him elected, and as a result he would become the first Democratic governor of Hawaii to lose his bid for a second term.

Shortly after the primary, David Ige and I sat down for a meeting. Though most of our conversation centered on the future of the utility industry, the real purpose was to feel each other out and see how we could work together once he took office. Though everyone expected him to win, the truth was Ige needed my support, especially since I had originally backed Governor Abercrombie's run for reelection.

This put me at odds with most of my union counterparts. Back in 2010, Abercrombie had run on a prolabor platform—tagline "A New Day"—and in return labor had thrown its considerable weight behind him. But, like so many politicians, once in office he discovered the real-life ramifications of his campaign slogans. Faced with an inherited fiscal disaster, he advocated several arguably practical and highly unpopular belt-tightening measures. He proposed a tax on the pensions of retirees, which didn't pass but earned him the reputation of being insensitive toward people on a fixed income. The nearly thirteen-thousand members of the Hawaii State Teachers Association were enraged when he proposed a contract that cut salaries and benefits while instituting more stringent teacher evaluations. After a heated battle that included a lawsuit, the matter was resolved in the teachers' favor, but the damage to Abercrombie had already been done. The HSTA threw their support—and $140,000 in political ads—behind Ige.

There was also a very public showdown with the Hawaii Government Employees Association, specifically public-sector nurses, over a proposed cut in their pay. After explaining that he had actually been trying to get them more money, Abercrombie asked a nurse, "Where is your leadership?" He was referring to the heads of the HGEA. The video of the exchange went viral, adding to the heap of negative media coverage that painted Abercrombie as an angry man reneging on his promises. Having observed the adversarial manner in which some union guys approached negotiations, I could see the governor's point.

At the end of the day, however, it was probably his, "I'm not your pal," comment that cost him the election. In February of 2011, shortly before I decided to run for business manager, the governor proposed a cut in public workers' Medicaid reimbursements. When challenged about the measure, he replied, "I'm not your pal. I'm not your counselor. I am the governor. And I am determined to be truthful with everybody about what we have to do together to survive." And later, in a 2013 speech, he said that while he "would not abandon collective bargaining," he was also not going to let labor unions "bankrupt the future for all by buying some temporary solution that does not address the fundamental fiscal issues we cannot escape." While I felt he could have gotten his point across with less incendiary statements, I admired his willingness to put himself out there, even at the cost of political capital. I also agreed with much of what he said. After decades of fiscal mismanagement, he was declaring his intention to do whatever it took to get the state back on track, even if it was unpopular with the special interest groups who had elected him. He was also not going to sugarcoat the situation or hide behind political platitudes. It was what I had deal with, albeit on a much smaller scale, when I became business manager. And just as the original executive board did not want to listen to me, labor folks turned a deaf ear to Abercrombie. All they heard was someone they'd help put in power taking away their fringe benefits. They did not want to see that for the state to be solvent in the future, tough choices had to be made now. Democrats in Hawaii largely rejected this notion, and their choice in the primary largely influenced my own. Despite running for governor in a heavily union state, Republican Duke Aiona did not even claim to have any allegiance to labor, not to mention his conservative stance on social issues. Ige's other opponent, former Honolulu mayor and Independent Mufi Hannemann, might have been a good choice, but like Aiona he trailed on all of the polls. David Ige was clearly the best choice for the members, and I threw Local 1260's full support behind him.

• • •

Though the two Russells shared several traits undesirable in an employee, they had little else in common. Russell Yamanoha was incompetent and self-absorbed but otherwise harmless, while Takemoto's alcohol and anger issues reached new heights. Yamanoha often found himself the victim of Takemoto's aggression, and in November 2014, their animosity came to a head, and at the most inopportune moment. On the night of the gubernatorial election, I, along with several of my staff, attended a party to watch the returns. After the excitement of the primary, it was a rather anticlimactic event. Hawaii's government was—and still is—controlled by Democrats, and Ige was a shoo-in. At final count, he garnered 49.5% of the vote to defeat Aiona and Hannemann and become the eighth governor of Hawaii.

The election-night party was jam-packed with Ige supporters and detractors alike, as well as several local media outlets. They circled the event like hungry sharks, looking to interview the various politicos and other stakeholders—including local unions—directly affected by Ige's victory. I made my rounds as well, shaking hands with this one, stopping to chat with that one. Frivolous as it seemed, attending these events was one of the most critical parts of my job, as they presented opportunities to strengthen existing friendships and forge new ones in a "casual" atmosphere. They could also be tricky to navigate; you never knew whether you were snubbing the next power player or schmoozing the next social pariah.

I wasn't paying much attention to what the Russells were doing, though I noticed the ever-present glass of clear liquid in Takemoto's hand. Vodka had always been his favorite poison.

It wasn't until I was giving an on-camera interview that I noticed Takemoto and Yamanoha; they stood face-to-face and dangerously close to one another. Takemoto had an expression I knew all too well: drunk and angry. Yamanoha looked like a scared rabbit.

My eyes flicked back and forth between the Russells and the reporter, praying she wouldn't see them. I could already imagine the front page of the local paper with the headline: Gov's Party Interrupted by Union Brawl. It was not the way I wished to begin my relationship with the new administration.

Fortunately, the interview was coming to a close. As soon as the reporter walked away, I went over and pulled them aside like children fighting in the sandbox.

"What's going on with you two?"

"He's trying to hurt me," Yamanoha said.

I turned to Takemoto. "What's the matter with you?"

Watery eyes stared at me defiantly. "I don't like his tone."

"Well, stand down," I said, trying to keep my own face as congenial as possible so as not to draw more attention to us. "This is a work event, and there are a ton of people here. Go home."

They slinked off in opposite directions, and I was once again left wondering how I could have chosen such a staff.

• • •

One of the issues on which I disagreed with Governor-elect Ige involved the proposed buyout of Hawaiian Electric by NextEra, an energy giant with tentacles around the globe.

Talks of the buyout were made public in December 2014, after my conversation with Ige. At first I publicly opposed the sale, not because I didn't believe the company would bring value to the state, but because I wanted to gain leverage over them. Based in Florida, NextEra owned Florida Power and Light as well as many other energy companies around the country. NextEra promised to reduce Hawaii's exorbitant energy rates; they also claimed that the massive influx of cash they brought to the economy would help fix the overtaxed and antiquated infrastructure in preparation for the state's ambitious renewable energy goals. While this all sounded like the answer to a prayer, I initially viewed it with some skepticism. Unlike most of my union counterparts, I had never viewed companies as inherently "bad," but that didn't mean I blindly accepted whatever they said, either. It was like that remark my father had made all those years ago: "Beware of white men bearing gifts"; all I had to do was substitute "white" with "multinational corporations." There was a very real possibility that NextEra would steamroll, not only the Local 1260 members currently working for Hawaiian Electric, but the next generation of potential employees. One potential casualty was the call center, with the staggered wage rates I had worked so hard to negotiate three years earlier. What was to stop NextEra from deciding the center was redundant? They could shut us down and simply route the calls through one of their other facilities. I also had no idea how amenable NextEra would be to working with a union, and before I supported any deal I had to make sure workers were protected.

I also felt an obligation to the community at large; Hawaii's residents deserved to have the best energy product possible and at rates they could afford. Though I had nothing to do with the actual decision-making process, I was in a position to exert some pressure on those who did. If the recent gubernatorial election had proven anything, it was the continuing influence labor had on the goings-on in the state. Every time some local media outfit called for an interview—and it was quite often—I would simply reply, "Local 1260 does not support the deal at this time."

Privately, though, I was beginning to get excited about the many potential benefits of the deal. Much like the sale of land had transformed the financial status of Local 1260, I believed the infusion of cash from NextEra could indeed transform the utility industry in the state of Hawaii. Before committing to anything, I did my research to see how NextEra's model could be reconciled with the environment in Hawaii. I was also curious to see how NextEra functioned in other states, particularly those less labor friendly than Hawaii. One of the company's main holdings was Florida Light & Power, which was an open shop. Unlike Hawaii, Florida is a right-to-work state, meaning an employer could not condition employment on one's membership in a union. Having seen the difference between members actively involved in the union and those who grudgingly paid their mandatory dues, I long believed that open shops should be the norm. The only way for the labor movement to reverse its decline and begin to grow was to give workers, especially the younger generations, real incentives to join and give them the choice of whether to do so. Though I had never publicly advocated this—to do so would be professional suicide—I had created a model based on this view. Local 1260 was no longer about just battling employers for low-hanging fruit, but about sustainability and becoming an integral part of the community. It was a model that would work just as well in a right-to-work state as in one that made union membership mandatory.

That said, my views on the NextEra deal would ultimately be based not on my political views, but on what would most benefit members in the current climate. I sent Lisa Lorenzo to Florida to get a sense of how the company ran in a semi-union environment. She toured the Florida Power & Light facility, spoke to the employees, and returned with a comprehensive evaluation that would help inform my decision.

The next step was to sit down with the company and see for myself what they had to offer, and at what cost. By that time, they were more than willing to meet with us, and to prove it, they sent the CEO of their Hawaii Division and vice president of labor relations. I asked Brandon to join me at the meeting. After years of dealing with Takemoto's incompetence, I had asked Brandon to step in as chief of staff, and it was important for him to be there; plus, his years as a journeyman gave him a wealth of practical knowledge I would find useful when negotiating with NextEra's people. From the outset, they made it clear that the company was serious about doing business with the state of Hawaii, had the capacity and intention to bring benefits to the state, and was willing to work with the business.

The agreement had to be forward-thinking in terms of technology. No doubt the utility industry was changing, and rapidly. Solar City had merged with Tesla, and had created commercial solar panels that would reduce the consumption of fossil fuels by 1.6 billion gallons per year. This sort of work fell under Damien's jurisdiction.

Tesla had also figured out a way to use solar panels and battery storage modules. They could soak up the power provided by the sun throughout the day and hold onto that power to use as needed instead of oil. In the future, plants would look different, and the work done within them would be different. Like it or not, we had to move toward or be left behind forever. It was, to me, symbolic of the labor movement itself.

Within a few days, we had hammered out a deal we all felt comfortable with. The signed agreement stipulated that if the sale went through, there would be no layoffs of any kind for two years. They also assuaged my concerns about the call center, which would be integrated with others around the country. NextEra also agreed that if they contracted overhead and underground electrical work (which was done by lineman), they would look at workers from both Locals 1260 and 1186 first. This, with the understanding that the locals would come in with a competitive bid. This was not a green light to fleece the company. Of course, the whole thing was contingent upon the sale going through. If it did not, the whole thing would be moot, and the gentleman's agreement with Hawaiian Electric would still be in play.

When Damien Kim heard that I had taken care of him with NextEra, he was genuinely grateful. My own staff, however, had mixed reviews about the agreement. Sure, they smiled and congratulated me when I presented the idea at the staff meeting, and some of them even meant it. But when I looked at the faces of Russell Takemoto, Michael Brittain, and Amy Ejercito, I could tell they were annoyed that they had not been part of the negotiations. This, from people who barely came to work! I pointed out that they had only sent two high-level people, and it would have been inappropriate for us to go in like some sort of SWAT team. We didn't need a macho show of power but the kind of negotiating skills I had been trying to teach them for the past three years. I also didn't trust any of them to be in the negotiation room, but I refrained from saying so. It wouldn't do any good, and I saw no point in aggravating them further.

The state, however, including David Ige, remained opposed to the sale. Ige believed NextEra would not be able to handle the renewables. Others had different reasons; mostly, they didn't like the idea of a conglomerate from the mainland getting its hooks into Hawaii. I pointed out that mainland-based companies operated on Hawaii. Would they get rid of them as well to become an isolationist society? To me, something else was at work here: much like the myopia of labor when it came to change, it seemed those in local government would rather remain stagnant and simply attempt to control the decline rather than invite in something new that could create the opportunity for prosperity. They were also not happy that I was in favor of the sale.

I was most surprised by the lukewarm reaction from many of Hawaiian Electric's employees. It wasn't that they didn't agree with the terms, they just thought it was unnecessary to put them in writing. "They need us," I heard more than once, and the ignorance of the statement made me cringe. It was this sort of stale thinking that would lead to the loss of their jobs and put the American dream further out of reach.

I spoke to them about embracing change, once again using the Kauai meter readers as an example. "They have remote meter reading now," I said. "A signal travels from the meter at someone's home to the data bank at their headquarters. There is no need for the person to go out there." Per my agreement with Hawaiian Electric, those people had been transitioned into new skills within the company. That clause had also been included in the signed agreement with NextEra. This was not about forcing them, but about providing an opportunity. If an older person wanted to stay in their position until retirement, fine; however, it was imperative that younger people with years of work ahead of them learn to roll with the times. With technology moving faster than we could catch up with it, this was the only way to ensure that workers would remain gainfully employed.

• • •

One of the most important aspects of the new model for Local 1260 was community involvement. This was not only a political move, but a way to reintegrate labor into the society it served. After fighting for so long to get my staff to do their jobs, it was a true joy to see how quickly they—and the members—jumped at the chance to serve those less fortunate.

Each week the staff would spend an afternoon serving meals at the River of Life, an organization in downtown Honolulu that helped the homeless. They donated their own money to Aloha United Way and Shriner's, a hospital that served children with severe orthopedic issues. We also continued to hold charity golf tournaments, with the proceeds going to various worthy causes throughout the state.

No one, however, did more than union member Mark Staskow and his wife. Each year, they would travel to a remote, impoverished village in South America. Mark knew about water filtration, and he showed the people how to construct a simple water system so they could access clean water. His wife, who was a nurse and also belonged to a union, provided natives with basic medical care such as checkups and inoculations. The Staskows were grateful for the union salaries and vacation policies that allowed them to take three weeks off, and they were so inspired by Local 1260's work in the community that they took these trips under the auspices of the union, even though they paid their own way.

When "Living 808," a morning show on local Fox affiliate KHON, heard about the Staskows' good works, they decided to do a story on them. That was the beginning of a monthly spot, "Living 1260," that highlighted members' contributions to the community and their sense of *ohana,* a Hawaiian term for family that stretched far beyond blood relations. Getting the show was an incredible achievement, made even sweeter by the fact that eight of the forty Local 1260 members who were employed at the station got to work on it.

The success of these programs was due almost entirely to Marilyn. She also brought another revenue stream to Local 1260. As one of the most beautiful places on earth, Hawaii is regularly the site of television shows, films, and commercials. Historically, that work had been under the purview of the union; however, over the years, thanks to exorbitant union rates and lack of representation, much of that firm work had gone to Japan. Marilyn worked with the Hawaii Film Association to get many of those projects back to Hawaii. For each job that came, Local 1260 got a cut.

• • •

In 2015, two events changed the course of Local 1260. The first was when I decided to make Brandon my chief of staff. After years of begging him to do his job, I simply could not tolerate Russell Takemoto in that position any longer. Actually, I couldn't tolerate him at all, but I still could not bring myself to fire him. Instead of being grateful, however, Takemoto was furious. It wasn't that he cared so much about not being chief of staff anymore, he was more concerned that his salary had been reduced from $145,000 to $140, 000 a year . . . for doing *nothing*. I had succeeded, finally, in making an enemy of Russell.

The other event concerned the election of John O'Rourke, former business manager of Local 6 in San Francisco, to vice president of the Ninth District after my friend and colleague Mike Mowrey was pushed out. O'Rourke left Local 6 under investigation for fiscal impropriety, but this was swept under the rug because he was white, Irish, and Catholic.

Harold Dias wasted no time in kissing up to the new VP, and I was once again reminded that though Harold was not my boss, he had the right friends and would continue to throw his weight around. Play ball, or they will make you pay.

One day Harold called to tell me that O'Rourke was coming to Hawaii—something about "showing his support for the locals."

"I need you to set up a meeting between O'Rourke and Hawaiian Electric," he said. It sounded like more of an order than a request.

Now, I dealt with Hawaiian Electric every day, so I knew they had upcoming meetings with their board of directors.

"They're tied up that week, but I could set up meetings for you and John to meet with the television stations we rep."

Harold was adamant. "No, it has to be Hawaiian Electric."

When I told him there was nothing I could do, he called the company himself, even though he knew he was supposed to go through the business manager. The secretary set up the meeting, then immediately called Leeann to give her a heads-up. His breach of protocol didn't bother me so much as the idea that he could ruin my relationship with the company.

"I told you they don't have time," I told him. "They're just doing this as a favor to me."

"Well, they better make time," Harold snapped. "This is the vice president."

It took some effort, but I managed to keep myself from laughing. In what universe did Harold think a visit from a union VP would be a priority for the head of a major utility company?

It made me glad I had a conflict with my own schedule. I sent Brandon in my stead, which Harold was none too pleased about. When my son recounted the story to me later, I didn't bother to control my amusement. This all-important meeting had lasted three minutes and focused on the important issue of whether the company and the union would be holding a linemen rodeo. We had done one once before, and it apparently was quite popular.

"We'll certainly talk to Brian about it," the CEO had said congenially.

"Oh," Harold had said. "You can work directly with me."

His statement was curious; Harold wasn't one to volunteer his services, so I figured he either wanted to look good in front of John or usurp my relationship with the company.

Initially, I found O'Rourke to be cordial, if a little rigid. Shortly after he took office, I, along with Marilyn and other members of the staff, took a trip to Japan to negotiate bringing broadcast media jobs back to Hawaii. I was pretty sure O'Rourke wasn't experienced in this kind of work, and I *knew* Harold certainly wasn't, so I didn't ask them to come along. With the aid of a translator, I pitched Japanese executives on the idea of shooting movies and commercials there, and despite the language barrier, they were clearly amenable to working with us. The trip was a great success; we returned home with more work for our freelance photojournalists and other Hawaii International Film Association workers who were part of Local 1260.

Chapter 24

The year 2015 also brought more structural changes to the union. When I proposed an increase in union dues, people probably thought I was nuts. I had a rationale behind it, though, and it was the same as when I cut expenses. I was working to improve the fiscal health of Local 1260 and give us leverage in case we needed to take some sort of economic action (i.e. a strike).

At the next meeting, I outlined my plan for the increase. In addition to the financial cushion, it would also help fund scholarships and other community outreach efforts, as well as purchases on behalf of the members. Finally, it would pay for the Local 1260 75th Anniversary gala, which would be free to members.

While we were, in many respects, moving forward as an organization, I was still dealing with the mistakes of staff members who, if not for their utter incompetence, I might have believed were trying to undermine my efforts.

Lisa Lorenzo, for example, was in charge of the customer service area—or call center—of Hawaiian Electric. Unfortunately, she was fiercely hated by members, for the simple fact that she did not do her job. Hawaiian Electric's employees did not need someone to blow smoke up their asses and spew platitudes; they wanted an advocate. I realized the depth of their disdain when I walked into a dues meeting and heard a woman yelling and screaming. It seemed someone was always yelling and screaming about something at these meetings; sometimes, they were just griping, and other times, like now, I had to admit they had a point. We were asking them to dig deeper into their pockets, and they wanted to know what they were paying for.

"What's the matter?" I asked her.

"You guys are not worth a dues increase!"

"*I'm* not?"

"Well, you are," she conceded, "but the rest of your staff is not worth it."

This was one of those incredibly uncomfortable moments when I was forced to choose between BS-ing the members—which I refused to do—and admitting that some members of my staff were woefully inadequate. Since I could not very well do that, either, I chose a third option: humor.

"Well, you may have a point there." I waited for the short, rather cynical burst of laughter to subside, then spent a few minutes talking about the things my staff had accomplished. "You know you can always talk to me," I added.

The woman calmed down, and she even called after the meeting to thank me. Still, her words had hit home. Though we had made so many positive changes—things that would have taken someone else ten or fifteen years—there was still so much to be done. The woman at the meeting had reminded me that I would never fully realize my plan with my current staff. Though I'd never considered myself a naïve person, it had taken me quite a while to see that it was more than a lack of ability on their part; it was a lack of caring. You can teach a person the former, but not the latter.

Even after all my years in labor, I never ceased to be shocked by how cold some people could be. How could someone be working for a "movement" supposedly committed to social justice, yet have no interest in helping people? I saw Russell Yamanoha's true colors while at a conference in Miami. We had pulled into a store parking when I noticed a man standing next to his car, staring down at a flat tire. A few feet away a woman and a little girl sat forlornly on a bench.

I was about to get out of the car when I heard Russell whine, "Why do we have to stop?"

My head jerked up in surprise. Leeann and Jennifer were with us, and although they didn't say anything, I knew they were as disgusted as I was.

"Never mind," I muttered as I got our jack out of the trunk and walked over to help them put the tire on. The man could barely speak English but managed to convey his gratitude with an enthusiastic *gracias*. Eventually, and with clear reluctance, Russell eventually came over to help. When we were done, I handed the man forty dollars to help him with the repairs.

"What if that was your daughters or your wife?"

Russell stared at me as if I had three heads. "Yeah, yeah," he said finally, "I see what you're saying."

It was moments like those that I wondered if God was telling me to get out of the game altogether.

If not, why would He surround me with people who so clearly did not care about what I was trying to do?

One of Amy's responsibilities was to service the contracts at the Pacific Missile Range facility; in this regard, she was like any other rep serving as liaison between the company and Local 1260 members who worked there. I knew she wasn't as suited for the job as Teresa, who with time would have made an excellent rep. Teresa was also a much better attorney. But there was no point in comparing the two. Despite her shortcomings, I did not micromanage Amy's day to day. All I asked was that she build and maintain a strong relationship with the company, make herself available to the members, and keep me posted on what was going on. For the most part she communicated with them by phone or email, though she did fly to Kauai once or twice a month to meet with them in person. I also went once a quarter to show my face and let them know I was still engaged.

It wasn't long before I realized that Amy's idea of having a relationship with the company was arguing with them, and often over tedious details that were at best secondary to the main purpose and at worst, frivolous. When she couldn't get her way at the negotiating table, she was quick to send the matter off to arbitration, which of course defeated the purpose of having an attorney on staff. To me arbitration was like calling a strike; it was a tool to be used as a last resort when communication had completely broken down. And in my experience, communication rarely broke down when both parties were willing to listen to each other. When a disagreement arose, I would much rather pick up the phone and talk things out myself, which not only saved the members $40,000 but offered another opportunity to strengthen the relationship with the company. More importantly, it demonstrated true leadership, someone that would go to the mat for members, not let the chips fall where they may or rely on a third party who didn't even want the union to step in.

Things came to a head when Local 1260 was renegotiating Exelis's contract. In keeping with my promise to personally handle all Local 1260s contracts, I flew to Kauai to meet with Anthony Pererra, Mike Murray, and David Finn—who represented Exelis. All three men were union members working for the company, and I respected them all deeply. In fact, I would eventually bring David Finn over to work for me as an Outer Island representative. Amy was present for some of the meetings, but mainly as an observer.

Although organizing had paved my way for much of my career, I had come to see contract negotiations as the most important part of my role at the union. This had evolved along with my attitude about unions in general. For years I had been passionate about organizing because it was an opportunity to win over the hearts and minds of workers, so they could see the benefits of unionizing. As I'd watched those benefits dwindle, I'd shifted my focus to strengthening the existing relationships between our members and their employers for the benefit of both. I also thoroughly enjoyed the work.

That said, negotiation was sometimes tense and often downright draining. After months of back and forth, I left at eleven thirty one night, exhausted but trusting we had finally reached an agreement I believed the members would accept. When I came in the next day to tie up loose ends, I was in for a surprise.

"Brian," one of the company guys said, "we're set to close, but Amy is not on board." He lowered his voice a bit. "She does not know what she's doing."

I raised an eyebrow at him, then we returned to the table.

"From my side, Local 1260 agrees with the package. We will do our best to get this ratified."

We were just about to sign when Amy yelled across the table, "Wait, wait, I am not in agreement!"

Everyone at the table turned to look at her in surprise. I gave her a look as if to say, "Sister, you work for me."

If she understood what I was trying to communicate, she gave no indication. Instead she rattled on about section this and article that. Her point would have been a valid one, had it not pertained only to one member, when a total of five hundred would be affected by the deal. Her statement was ludicrous.

"Like I said, Local 1260 agrees with this package. Amy, I will see you outside."

She got up and followed me to the hall. "Amy," I said when we were out of earshot, "don't you ever do that again. You are undermining me and the entire process."

"But Brian, we need this covered."

"This is one thing with one guy. I can close this right now."

The one guy had tested dirty on one of the company's random drug tests. Why Amy thought his case was worth holding up the whole deal, I had no idea. I suspected, though, that she was letting her ego do the negotiating for her. It was a common enough problem in such situations, and I had tried like hell to train my staff not to indulge. "It's very simple," I would tell them. "Listen to each other with your heart; it makes all the difference in the world." When it came to Amy, I had clearly been wasting my breath.

When she refused to budge, I called the project manager, "Z," and Bruce Collier, who was negotiating on the company side, along with a federal negotiator.

"Okay," I said to him. "Tell me what he did." Though I knew it already, I gave Z the respect of asking for his perspective. Sure enough, the guy had been caught with drugs in his system.

"I want to bring this guy back to work." I looked at him. "Can we do this? Can we bring him back?"

Z shrugged. "Why should we?"

I saw his point; on the other hand, I hated to see an otherwise good worker lose his livelihood over a mistake. Most of all, I wanted the agreement settled once and for all. The other members had waited long enough.

"Here's what I see, Z. I see you giving him another chance. What if he is clean for six months? Then he comes back, with his seniority intact."

"No," Z said, shaking his head. "He comes back as a new employee."

"C'mon, Z, you have nothing to lose. The guy has ten years in and a family—everything to lose. If he screws up, you put him out on the street. But if you give him a chance and he blossoms, you'll have a loyal employee for life."

Z thought for a minute. "Two years?"

I smiled. "How about if he tests clean for a year, he gets his seniority back. If he doesn't test clean, he shouldn't be here anyway."

Z agreed, thereby settling a point that Amy had been arguing with them for six months. The man she was so concerned about had been out of work the whole time. If she was really interested in helping, she could have compromised.

This was perhaps the most frustrating aspect of my time in office. Since becoming business manager, one of my goals had been to show my staff the proper way to negotiate. Yes, you enter into a negotiation with what you want or need; however, once you're sitting at that table, you must really listen to what the other side has to say, look at the situation as objectively as possible, and try to meet them in the middle. Sometimes, as difficult as it may seem, you must go all the way to the other side in order to give them what is most important on their agenda. This was not about simple horse-trading, or being a bully or a wimp, I told them, for those labels had no place in true arm's-length discussion. Instead, it was about building relationships out of genuine respect and understanding.

My ways were completely contrary to the way labor had always interacted with employers; they also required a great deal of introspection, for to be a successful negotiator, one must put their ego aside and understand their role as a facilitator of a process.

For me, this process was successful when it resulted in safe, responsible, profitable workplaces that fostered mutual respect and responsibility between employers and employees. From where I stood, labor had originally been a valuable advocate for workers but for decades had stood in the way of this partnership. They painted corporations as evil when the reality was that they were major players in American success. From what I had seen of unions, all they saw were the dues they collected. Here they were supposed to be protecting the American worker, and instead they created drama to protect themselves. It never even occurred to them that the American dream should be equally attainable by corporations and employees; nor did they realize that while more difficult than self-righteously fist-pounding on the table, conversations founded in equality were much more effective.

At some point, I had to admit that no matter how much I worked with them, most of my staff had neither the skills nor the desire to operate in such a manner. Despite how things had ended after the Tommy Decano incident, Teresa Morrison did have the potential to be a highly effective negotiator. Amy, on the other hand, was another sort entirely. Her training as an attorney had handicapped her in this regard. She would get caught up in doing battle with the company, even if it meant the matter ended in arbitration. I was completely against this, unless there was no other option; it was a sign of laziness and an admission of defeat. The members wanted to see leadership, not someone who hid behind their title, then threw everything up in the air and relied on a third party, all to the tune of $40,000.

Other members, this time from Hawaiian Electric, also expressed their dissatisfaction with Amy. That year, a huge scandal rocked the company when a female employee accused a group of men on the line crew of sexual assault. Normally, Amy would have been charged with their representation, but the members called the office and told Brandon they did not want her there; they did not trust her. Brandon didn't ask why they didn't trust her; we all knew she hadn't gone out of her way to form a relationship with them.

He stopped at my office before heading over. "You should come too. These guys know you; they are your generation."

After a moment, I nodded. Though I had no doubt Brandon could handle it without me, the men needed the type of moral support they could only get from a peer. They had to be terrified; it was their word against the woman, and their jobs, medical coverage—many even their freedom—was on the line.

Sure enough, the men thanked me for making the time to come. There was an investigation, then a settlement was reached between the woman and the company. I cannot speak to the particulars, but I can say the outcome, if not exactly ideal, was the best-case scenario.

Chapter 25

Each day, I pushed myself a little further than I had the day before, whether it was to bail out some employee at risk of losing his job or a member of my own staff risking all the goodwill we had built in the community. I felt a constant sense of urgency, a need to complete things before the other shoe dropped. What the other shoe was, I had no idea.

The responsibility of running Local 1260 was draining my family as well. They told me several times that eventually something would have to give, not just for my sake, but for theirs as well. Even Brandon, who was only in his early thirties, said more than once, "Dad, I cannot do this forever. I cannot keep up this pace."

I couldn't argue with him there. We were all together twenty-four hours a day, whether at work or at home, eating, sleeping, and breathing Local 1260. A lot of families would have resented me, or completely crumbled under the pressure, and the fact that they didn't was nothing less than a gift from God.

One day, when Marilyn asked me how much longer I expected us all to do this, I told her of my new plan: I would finish out my second term, run and win again in 2017, then downsize. There would be no more coddling of the two Russells, Melanie, Michael Brittain, and his equally toxic friend, Dan Rose. All of them would go, as would Amy Ejercito. Having a lawyer on staff had once seemed so important. It wasn't worth it, though, if the lawyer we had only added more dead weight.

Much as she must have loathed the thought of four more years, Marilyn agreed. Through it all, she had been my rock. We promised each other that no matter how hairy things got, we would never let it affect our marriage, but there were many times when I felt like she was holding up my end of the bargain as well as her own.

There were moments when I picked up my head just long enough to acknowledge an accomplishment that really moved Local 1260 forward. One such milestone was the day I was finally able to start hiring Outer Island representatives. The first was my longtime ally and former executive board member, Kris Hoke. After her term as president, in 2014 she had run for and won the office of treasurer; then in January of 2015, at my invitation, she left the board altogether to rep members on the Big Island.

My choice for Kauai was also a no-brainer. David Finn had impressed me during the Pacific Missile Range negotiations, and he would turn out to be just as talented as an Outer Island rep. Like Kris on the Big Island, he met with members and their families, strengthening relationships and dramatically increasing representation. He also did a segment on Living 808, in which he talked about Local 1260's work with Big Brothers/Big Sisters. Both he and Kris did excellent work, which was a great relief, not only to me, but to Brandon, who as chief of staff was responsible for interfacing with them. Now, instead of us having to run to the various islands to put out fires, we were able to delegate such duties to their capable hands. I had no idea that merely a year later, all of their work would be thoughtlessly dismantled by those I thought were my friends.

• • •

I had always believed in taking the time to reevaluate my goals and assess how close I was to achieving them. Most of my first term as business manager had been spent correcting the mismanagement of the past and restructuring the finances of Local 1260. I wanted my second term to be about creating opportunities for existing members to advance their careers and having something to offer to the next generation of workers. Of all my goals, the two dearest to my heart were the construction training and media apprenticeship programs. They were also the most ambitious.

With its six-figure salary and highly specialized skills, the job of construction linemen was highly coveted. The problem was, there was only one way to become a lineman in the state of Hawaii, and that was through Hawaiian Electric. Since they only hired about twenty people a year, one had to be extremely lucky to get in. A training program would be a win-win—workers would more easily be able to survive in one of the most expensive states in the nation, and they would have an enormous incentive to join Local 1260. Like everything else I tried to do, it soon became mired in union politics.

From the first, Harold Dias was against the construction program; he wanted his pal Damien to have jurisdiction over outside construction. For Harold, it boiled down to who he could control, and whereas I had resisted his efforts, Damien had embraced them. When Damien lost his bid for reelection as business manager of Local 1186, Harold had claimed "employer intervention," which is against the law and therefore grounds for a do-over. The second time around, Damien magically won by seven votes, and Harold had someone in his back pocket. When Lonnie Stephenson, who succeeded Ed Hill as president of the IBEW, gave me jurisdiction over construction, Harold was furious, though it would be several months before I learned just how far he would go to exact his revenge. In the meantime, I was given the green light to set up the construction training program. We set aside space for our offices, and I planned on putting my daughter-in-law Neiani in charge of dispatch. For the time being, Russell Takemoto was there as well; I didn't believe for a minute he could handle it, but by then there was simply nowhere else left to put him.

The other program was for high school and college kids who had an interest in journalism, both in front of and behind the camera. Whether someone wanted to be an anchor or the "weather girl," they would now have a fully accredited program to learn their trade. In return, Local 1260 would make itself relevant to young people who otherwise would not have been aware of its existence.

• • •

By the beginning of 2016, the country was bracing for what would become the most contentious election year in modern American history. Over the next several months, friends and family would stop speaking, violence would erupt at political rallies, on social media and on college campuses, and it would become increasingly difficult to discern whether the news we were being inundated with was true or had been cooked up by one pot-stirrer or another.

Like most of the country, Hawaiians watched the unfolding drama with the same combination of fascination and disgust as they did *Keeping Up with the Kardashians*. They sat glued to their televisions as Donald Trump filleted his numerous (and arguably more qualified) Republican rivals and thought this was all just good theater. This reality show clown, who bragged about the size of his hands and hurled outlandish insults at, well, everyone, would never get the nomination. And even if he did, it didn't matter, because Hillary Clinton was a shoo-in for the White House. She had paid her dues and would ride the coattails of a highly popular president into office. The whole process seemed like little more than a formality.

Then came the Iowa caucus, followed by several primaries in which Trump was the victor. It was like a twenty-car pileup—surreal, scary, and impossible to ignore. Trump was vague on a number of topics, from healthcare to how he would defeat ISIS. He was clear, however, about his contempt for unions and their stronghold on the economy. Other Republicans said as much, but somehow, when Trump stated his intention to stir things up, people believed it. Hillary Clinton, on the other hand, would be a victory for the status quo for Washington,

DC, and Big Labor itself. With few exceptions, including the Fraternal Order of Police and the National Border Patrol Council, unions had thrown their considerable weight—and their wallets—behind Clinton.

As if things weren't tense enough, the country was dealt another blow on February 13, 2016, when Supreme Court Justice Antonin Scalia was found dead of an apparent heart attack. Scalia, who had been appointed to the court by President Ronald Reagan in 1986, was arguably the most influential—and the most conservative—in recent history, and everyone, regardless of whether they loved or hated his views, agreed that his vacant seat would throw the court into turmoil. It also significantly upped the ante with regard to the presidential election.

Of all the things a president can do to affect our lives, few are as impactful as the choosing of a justice. Though we may not think about it every day, the Supreme Court affects nearly every aspect of life, from abortion and marriage rights to interstate commerce and healthcare. Scalia's death left the court with only eight justices—and therefore the potential for deadlocked cases. It would come to symbolize the battle for the hearts and minds of the American people, and the case *Friedrichs v. California Teachers Association et al* exemplified that battle.

The issue in Friedrichs was whether to overturn the Abood decision of 1977. As mentioned earlier, Abood had created a distinction in union fees paid for collective bargaining and those paid for political activities. Public sector employees—even those who chose not to join the union—could be compelled to pay for the former, as they benefitted from the union's collective bargaining efforts in terms of salary, pension, medical benefits, et cetera. They could not, however, be forced to pay dues for the latter, as this was construed as forcing them to support political ideologies in violation of their First Amendment rights. The Friedrichs case sought to take this a step further by stating that any mandatory fees were in violation of such rights.

The lead plaintiff, Rebecca Friedrichs, was an Orange County elementary schoolteacher who, before bringing suit, had served on the executive board of her local union. She and nine other teachers represented by the Center for Individual Rights had paid the mandatory agency, or "fair share service fees," which were about the same amount as the regular union dues. They argued that collective bargaining was "inherently political," and cited an overly burdensome process they had to follow in order to opt out of paying for it.

The California Teachers Association (CTA) might have taken issue with the word inherently, but it did concede that 30 percent of the fees were used to finance political activities. The best example was CTA's fight against California's Proposition 75, which would have required employees' prior consent before using agency fees for political contributions. It went to the heart of the plaintiffs' claim that they were being forced to financial stances they did not agree with. Despite this, the Ninth Circuit Court stuck to the rationale of Abood, which was to strike a balance and prevent nonmembers from "freeloading," or reaping benefits of the union's collective bargaining efforts without paying for the service.

The case was argued before the Supreme Court in January, about a month before Scalia's death. He most certainly would have sided with the plaintiffs, and without him the court was split down the middle and along ideological lines. The real surprise came on March 29, when instead of waiting to see whether the Republicans confirmed Obama pick Judge Merrick B. Garland, the court issued a one-line per curiam decision upholding the Ninth Circuit's decision. Although the decision held no precedential value, Big Labor hailed this as a victory. As usual, they failed to see the handwriting on the wall—that this was really just a reprieve, the length of which depended upon who won the presidential election and therefore put a new justice in place. One thing was clear, the Center for Individual Rights and other conservative groups were not going to take this lying down. They would keep bringing such cases until mandatory fees were a thing of the past.

As a lifelong Democrat, I too supported Hillary. In my opinion, she not only had the brains but the political chops for the job. That said, my decision to vote for her was not because of her policies on labor, but in spite of them. If my experience told me anything, a commitment to labor had little to do with workers and everything to do with preserving the present structure that disempowered them. If I were voting purely on the union issue, I might have made another choice. But Election Day was still months away, and for the time being I was like everyone else, watching an exciting if trashy movie of which I already knew the ending.

As the nation descended into chaos, Local 1260 was finally getting into a rhythm. At the first staff meeting of 2016 I handed everyone new business cards—the result of the rebranding project I had begun a few months earlier. Local 1260's logo, a fist with a lightning bolt, had been revamped and the new tagline, "Organizing the Future," added. To me, it captured the feeling of pride for all we had accomplished, as well as hope and optimism for what was to come. This included the construction and media programs, both of which were on their way to becoming a reality. And in March, Local 1260 made IBEW history once again, this time for the first long-distance organizing campaign. When the email from the firefighters came through, I was terribly excited, not just because they were interested in learning more about the union, but because they were from Wake Island. As Wake Island was in the middle of the Pacific and a five-hour plane ride from Hawaii, it was clear that this was a result of my social media outreach. I never learned whether it was a Facebook post or a YouTube video, but it didn't matter, so long as they were inspired. I turned it over to Brandon, who communicated the vision of Local 1260 more eloquently over Skype than most would in person. The win was touted by the International, not only as an amazing accomplishment, but as a sort of admonishment for the rest of the union. No one, they said, could ever make an excuse as to why they couldn't organize, not when Local 1260 had done so from thousands of miles away! It was even written up in the IBEW monthly newsletter, and added to our list of winning campaigns in the construction, broadcasting and media, and utility jurisdictions.

Only John O'Rourke seemed singularly unimpressed.

"Why would you bother to organize twelve guys?" he said when I told him about Wake Island.

"They want to be in the IBEW."

"I want to see the hundred, two-hundred, five-hundred-man campaigns."

"Well, if that was the mentality in 1890, we wouldn't be here right now."

It was a reference to the IBEW's humble beginnings in St. Louis, Missouri, in the late nineteenth century. While in St. Louis for an expo on electricity, ten disgruntled electrical workers met with an AFL organizer at Stolley Dance Hall. A year later, in 1891, the International Brotherhood of Electrical Workers was born.

John paused. "Oh, I see what you're saying . . . "

There was nothing in his tone to indicate that he was annoyed—in fact, he sounded a bit sheepish—but I knew my comment had hit its mark. It was one of those conversations that seemed so innocuous at the time but later proved to be indicative of a person's mindset and motivation.

• • •

That same month, I brought my son-in-law Eric on board to work in the new construction department. Eric was an extremely hard worker and as skilled a journeyman as I had ever seen, and I trusted him completely with this next leg of our expansion. For his part, Eric was excited about getting in on the ground floor of this venture, so much so that he was willing to leave a comfortable job and move Megan and the kids out west, all on his own dime. I knew this was a sore spot for Harold Dias—he didn't like that I was organizing groups he hadn't gone near for twenty years—but he said nothing about me hiring Eric. No one said anything, which is what made what happened two months later all the more shocking.

• • •

A central feature of my vision for Local 1260 and, by extension labor in general, was a reintegration into mainstream society. I recalled the prominent role the union had played during my father's era, and was deeply saddened by its descent into irrelevance in recent decades. I strongly believed that labor could once again be a force for good in the community. To do this, however, the leadership would have to do two things: return to their ideological roots as a movement working for the betterment of the American middle class, and be forward-thinking in terms of their processes, procedures, and willingness to adapt to the times.

In just a few short years, Local 1260 had come close to fulfilling that vision. No longer were we despised, as was the case after the storm and strike of 2011; in fact we had built a recognizable brand throughout Hawaii. We paid for local television commercials that showcased our contribution to the state, including our commitment to uplifting the community. We also sponsored the Skycam that glided over the Honolulu skyline during the news each evening. No matter how many times I saw this, I never tired of seeing the tagline that appeared at the top of the screen: "Brought to you by IBEW Local 1260, along with our newly designed logo." Not only was the tagline evidence of the improved relationship between the community and the union; it also built morale among the members. It gave me an immense sense of satisfaction to know that they were seeing it on TV and thinking, "That's my union. I'm with them." It was only there for a few seconds, but it communicated a feeling of belonging to something bigger than themselves.

Chapter 26

Word of the changes at Local 1260 had also spread to the mainland. I was deeply honored when the Federal Mediators Conciliation Services invited me to speak at their annual conference in Chicago. I would be addressing a crowd of about three thousand people on negotiating interest-based solutions, specifically as they applied to government contracts.

Over the years I had worked closely with federal mediators—they were present at the same Pacific Missile Range meetings that Amy nearly tanked, as well as various negotiations at Hawaiian Electric—and I had always been impressed with their professionalism and efficiency. The fact that they reached out to me was a testament to the fact that Local 1260 now had a model worth emulating.

The federal mediators and I shared the same philosophy, namely, that we were coming to the table, not merely to negotiate a compromise but to negotiate for consensus. This could only occur when each side was able to understand the other's interests and issues. They did not seek to meet in the middle, but would go all the way to view the situation from the other person's perspective.

While this may sound simple—even common sense—it is all too rare in the negotiating world, especially when it involves labor.

Whereas professional negotiators are by nature objective—they are trained to be so and have no stake in the outcome—lay negotiators must engage in a great deal of "mental hygiene." When both sides are invested (i.e. employee and employer), they must be willing to check their egos at the door; otherwise they will be so preoccupied with winning that they will be sure to lose. In trying to prove to the other side how much smarter and tougher they are, they will become sloppy in thought and word, and most likely concede something important. Negotiating well required introspection, evolution. Finally, it meant realizing that the world would be a better place if people—whether part of a company, a marriage, or a union—could communicate in a way that respected each other's autonomy and integrity, instead of assuming that the other party had dastardly motives.

This philosophy also encompassed a knowledge of self; in fact, this was a key component. For if we didn't know the self, how could we know what we truly wanted and why we fought so hard for it? How could we bring someone over to our side unless we truly believed what we advocated was beneficial and were willing to go out on a limb for it? As business manager, I had to live this philosophy every day. Whether it was contract negotiations with an employer or a proposed financial change to the structure of the union, I had to first deal with any outside parties—employers, investment firms, et cetera—then go to the members to explain the outcome. This was usually the toughest part; the rank and file were never privy to these discussions and understandably skeptical about what went on there. The rapport I built with them would go a long way to assuaging their concerns, but at the end of the day, if they didn't like what I was doing, they would simply vote me out the next election. I refused to let this influence what I did at the negotiating table or how I presented my case to the members. If I did, I would be no better than the rest of labor, dedicated only to protecting my fiefdom. I never sold anything to the members that I did not believe in 100 percent. So long as I explained it properly, the members would believe in it too.

The same was true for my staff. It didn't matter what I was working on or how frustrated I was with them—I always acted in what I believed was in their best interest and gave them a full explanation of what I did and the rationale behind it. Staff meetings were the forum for these discussions; they also provided an opportunity to take stock of what had already been accomplished, what still needed to be done, and most importantly, whether we were behaving in a manner that would benefit the members.

As mentioned earlier, this commitment was rooted in my spiritual beliefs, which were shared, at least in theory, by many of my staff. In these meetings I often relied on the words of Joel Osteen, whose style of ministering I found to be refreshing, easy to relate to, and often humorous. At what would turn out to be my last staff meeting as business manager, I recounted an anecdote from Osteen's most recent book, *Every Day a Friday*. It told the tale of two bricklayers in New York City. A man asked the first bricklayer what he did for a living, to which he shrugged and said, "I just lay one brick after another." When the man posed the question to the second bricklayer, his face lit up and he said, "I build enormous skyscrapers where people work and flourish." The point of the story of course was that while the two men did the exact same job, one did so just to collect a paycheck, while the other had passion and purpose—he knew that his labor had a positive impact on his community.

As I looked around the table and saw everyone nodding their heads in agreement, I believed the message had hit home. Just a few weeks later, several of these same people would be active, or at least complicit, in my removal from office and the character assassinations perpetrated against me and my family by the IBEW and the local media.

• • •

Around that same time, Amy Ejercito decided to retire from Local 1260. We threw her a party with drinks, a cake, and some gifts, and she offered everyone—including myself—what appeared to be heartfelt thanks for serving as her colleagues over the past few years. I was not especially sorry to see her go—working with her had more often than not been a frustrating experience—but as I watched her clean out her desk that last day, I sincerely wished her well. I was also relieved. She was one less person I would have to get rid of when I downsized the staff. I had no way of knowing that my time at Local 1260 was also numbered.

A few weeks later, on the morning of Friday, May 6, John O'Rourke and Harold Dias entered Local 1260's offices and in less than ten

minutes decimated my thirty-five-year career with the IBEW. It was
the strangest feeling as Marilyn and I walked out of the Topa Offices.
On the one hand I was numb and shell-shocked, almost incapable of
coherent thought; on the other hand, my mind raced. *How can they
do this to me? Why are they doing this to me? How do I fight it?* I
pulled out my phone and called everyone on the staff, asking them
to meet at a nearby park. Those who did show up looked as shocked
as I felt; those who didn't went straight to the office and started
working. Later, when the dust began to settle, I would realize those
who didn't show up had been in on it. I had given them the day off,
so why else would they have shown up at the office unless they knew
I no longer had authority over such things? Michael Brittain showed
me the courtesy of picking up the phone, only to patronize me by
playing dumb.

"I am a loyal soldier," he said when I told him what had happened.
Yes, but loyal to whom?

He then proceeded to unleash a litany of abuse that left my mouth
hanging open—things like, "You're an asshole, Brian"; "You were the
worst boss, Brian"—that sort of thing. With each insult, his voice got
louder and his language saltier.

I put the call on speaker phone so Marilyn, who sat next to me in
the car, could serve as my witness. In thirty-five years of marriage,
I had never seen my wife's eyes open so wide.

"What is wrong with you, Mike?" I asked him, struggling to keep
cool. After the morning I'd had, it was certainly a challenge.

"You read our fucking emails!"

I took a deep breath. "But Mike, you were working your side business at the office. The members are paying for your time, so when you're not working on their behalf, it's the equivalent of stealing from them. You do realize that, right?"

Michael went back to his ranting, but I knew I had him. Throughout his tenure at Local 1260, he spent a great deal of his time working on his digital design business when he should have been tending to the needs of members. Even worse, the software he used—a sort of computerized sketchpad—slowed down the office network. I learned of this after engaging an outside IT company to tell me why the brand-new computers I had purchased were operating at a crawl. Later I learned that he'd go around to other staff members and ask them to stop streaming for a couple of hours, though as a rep he had no authority to do so. They didn't know the reason for his request, but they did come to me and complain about him. So, yes, I had read his emails, as was within my right as business manager. I may not have had the heart to fire people, but I was going to know what they were doing during business hours.

"You're an asshole, Brian," he said again. "And whatever happens to you is going to happen to you." He always lashed out when he knew he was wrong, and as much as I wanted to put him in his place, I was not about to give him the satisfaction.

"Right, Michael, whatever you say."

My mind was reeling as I ended the call. Michael's reaction, while typical of him, was nonetheless telling. He was not surprised to hear about the trusteeship; in fact, it seemed as though he had been waiting for the chance to rub it in. I suddenly remembered how he'd gone around telling people that he was going to be the next business manager. The idea was laughable, and besides, why would he even want the job? It required actual work and left little time for ego and animosity toward others.

My suspicions were later confirmed by a letter from Local 1260 to its members that was leaked to the press. It "explained" the situation and cited those on the staff who could still be trusted. All those listed had been part of the conspiracy to oust me, or at least who knew about it. Michael Brittain's name was not that shocking; however, the identity of the letter's author was. Three days after Local 1260 was put under trusteeship, Amy Ejercito came out of "retirement" and was back at the office. Could the whole thing have been an act? Had she really accepted gifts and made flowery speeches knowing she would return after I was canned? As insane as it seemed, I reminded myself that I had seen worse.

Chapter 27

It would take me a while to piece together what had really happened, that my ouster was not as sudden as it seemed but had been meticulously and callously planned. For a few weeks, the onslaught from the local media took up all my attention. These so-called "journalists" left no stone unturned in their campaign to humiliate and villainize me. All the things that had made me so effective as business manager—my long history with the IBEW and the fact that I was a native Hawaiian and intimately knew the needs of its people—now made me a more appealing target. I had become one of those public figures who turned out to be a "crook."

During those first eight weeks or so, I questioned every professional choice I had ever made. I had done all this work—often pushing myself beyond my limits—only to have it destroyed by jealousy and greed. Maybe I should have just gone through the motions, done enough just to remain employed, but I knew myself enough to know this would never have worked. My feelings for Local 1260 and its members ran much deeper than just a job; I believed they were part of God's plan, but that didn't meant I let things roll off my back. It was a true dark night of the soul.

I had spent thirty-five years—my entire adult life—serving the IBEW, and my "retirement party" consisted of grab your stuff and get the hell out. It was not about looking for a reward or a pat on the back, but about feeling that my life had value. I had bought into the union as a brotherhood, and my "brothers" had just thrown me out like a piece of trash.

It seemed everywhere I looked, another accusation was being levelled at me. Suddenly everyone behaved as if I had acted unilaterally and in circumvention of the union bylaws and constitution. The lovely Kauai house, which was intended to resurrect the camaraderie I'd experienced in the union hall while growing up, now sat unused with the grass overgrown. The IBEW now claimed I had not gotten permission to buy it, that the office in the Topa Offices had been my one authorized purchase. One needed only to look at the lease agreement to see that this was yet another falsehood.

One of the International charges involved the staff trip to Hong Kong two months earlier. Interestingly, the IBEW charged me and my family with improprieties, but not the others travelling with us. This same trip would later be used by the IBEW at Brandon's unemployment hearing. After an investigation, the state of Hawaii found it to be a legitimate business trip, and he was allowed to collect.

The International even attacked my attempts to tighten the belt. I was genuinely flabbergasted when they alleged I had instituted pay cuts in order to benefit me and my family. How in the hell was that even possible? They charged me with using union funds to "buy food for my daughter." They did not mention, though, that Megan had opened her home to me and my staff while we attended a conference in DC. She did this not for personal gain but because she knew how important it was to me to save the members money. Local 1260 did not have to pay for a hotel, and the food I purchased was less expensive than going to a restaurant. It didn't matter how ludicrous the charge was, the International concocted and the media served them up, no evidence or corroboration needed.

The most ridiculous charge of all had to do with the *amount* of time I worked. The IBEW claimed that I had taken 171 days in unreported vacation time, time for which I now owed them money. Where had they gotten this number? From Russell Takemoto's girlfriend, Melanie Salvador. She was in charge of the books, and apparently she had noted each day I was out of the office. Of course she didn't bother to mention that I was not soaking up sun or—as members of my truant staff often did—playing a few rounds on the golf course—but running around like a chicken without a head. If I wasn't at a members' meeting in person, I attended via video conferencing; if I wasn't speaking to a CEO, I was discussing Local 1260's portfolio with an investment firm. There were times when—just as I had allowed my staff to do—I worked from home. Melanie knew this as well as anyone, but just as she had lied to cover up Russell's absences over the years, she now lied to further the conspiracy to which he was a part. If the next business manager also kept her on, all the better. The International, with this paranoid need to make sure everyone was chained to their desk, was easy to convince I was taking advantage. Fortunately, I had also documented everything I was doing, down to every last contract negotiation, interview, and charity event.

Melanie caused me other problems as well. While I had once considered her merely incompetent, I was now concerned that she had "cooked the books" to make it look like I had done wrong. She was the only person who handled Local 1260's finances; she had control of how much money was put into the various accounts. Like all the other staffers, I had given Melanie quite a bit of autonomy, and now I kicked myself for it. I had no idea what she did; all I knew was that I had been accused of financial wrongdoing, and she was still there. I thanked God for all the checks and balances we had, including quarterly and yearly audits. Had they not been in place, my enemies could have made God-knows-how much money disappear, then accused me of taking it.

As mentioned earlier, I did not even have the authority to sign checks—the president and treasurer of the executive board did that. When the local needed to issue a check, Melanie was the one who went to them to get it signed. I knew Ron Girard, who took over as president after Kris Hoke became an Outer Island rep, hadn't done anything unseemly; he was a decent guy and we worked well together. He also had nothing to gain from my removal. It all remained a mystery, including how Melanie had gotten her hands on the policies. The maintaining and protecting of important documents were the responsibility of the business manager; this included the database of all employees' names, addresses, and phone numbers, as well as the bylaws and the constitution. Local 1260's bylaws were made available on request, but as they were really just the nuances of how our office was run (i.e. how often staff members got paid), rarely did anyone request to see them. If someone had a question, I usually told them it was a policy (i.e. you get paid every other week).

I did have my suspicions, however. I never locked the individual office doors, so she easily could have gone in and made changes to the policies, then replaced them so the people from International who later cleaned out my office would assume I had done it. What they didn't know was that I had the real policies—those approved by the International back in 2013—in my bag. Leeann had a copy as well.

• • •

The media even reached out to Teresa Morrison, who had since moved to New Jersey. She remarked that she "could see me" doing what I had been accused of. I replayed her time at Local 1260 over and over again, wracking my brain for anything that could have given her these notions about me. I recalled the nice young woman who had worked with Marilyn and so impressed me with her passion and promise. I remembered recruiting her early in her legal career and taking her under my wing to teach her the ins and outs of negotiating labor contracts. I could not recall, however, anything that would lead her to believe that I was capable of fiscal mismanagement. Could this be some sort of payback for releasing Tommy four years earlier? Whatever her reasoning, it was like a dagger to the heart.

I actively watched the coverage for about a week, feeling sick to my stomach yet unable to turn it off. Even after I couldn't take it anymore,

I found myself bombarded with whatever erroneous story the IBEW had cooked up that day. More than once, Marilyn and I went to a diner for dinner and saw my face looking back at us from the newspaper vending machines by the front door. I'd stare, open-mouthed, unable to believe this was happening to me. Then I'd feel the gentle pressure of Marilyn's hand on my arm.

"Don't look, Brian; just don't look."

The problem was, everyone else was looking. As we ate our meal, I'd see people sitting there with their paper, glancing between me and the front page, trying to figure out if I was the guy.

I could have endured that, I think, had it not been for the vicious attacks leveled against my family. So-called "journalists" cited their salaries on television, in the papers, and online, even though I had paid them significantly less than was allowed by the bylaws. Every article and post depicted Marilyn, Brandon, and Neiani as talentless beneficiaries of my nepotism, even though historically, members of the same family often worked in the union. One example was the business manager of Local 47 in Southern California. He hired his daughter and two sons. Even John O'Rourke, when he headed a local, had hired his brother to work there. If the International fired everyone who engaged in such "nepotism," there would be no one left working there! It was a common, accepted, and even respected practice, so long as the people were qualified. In fact, when Ed Hill was president, he encouraged hiring within one's family, because it "bred loyalty." Once again he had gotten it wrong. For him, loyalty meant a political alliance to the person who had hired them. For my family, that loyalty also extended to the members. It was not about us, but the workers we served.

I thought of all the times I had looked at Marilyn, Brandon, and Neiani and knew they desperately needed a break but didn't take one because there was still more work to be done. I thought of the times Jennifer had taken that horrendous trip to Guam because she knew that in assisting Ken she'd be helping me keep my promise to the members there. I'd put my family in place because I knew they were qualified, committed, and trustworthy; and because after giving the other staffers several chances, I'd found them to be incompetent and apathetic. With their work ethic and experience Marilyn, Neiani, and Brandon could have done anything they wanted; they came to Local 1260 because they believed in the mission, so much so that they were willing to accept salaries on the low end of the scale set out in the bylaws. The media made much of the fact that Marilyn was paid $120,000, but according to our bylaws she could have made $150,000. Neiani could have made over $90,000; I paid her around $75,000. Brandon also made well below the amount allowable for the chief of staff position.

The International and journalists alike chose to ignore the fact that each member of my family was highly qualified for their position. No one wrote about Brandon's years as a journeyman, organizer, and shop steward; his organizing win on Wake Island, which had been touted just two months earlier, was now completely forgotten. When they wrote about Marilyn, it was not to talk about her liaising between Local 1260 and the charities, her community-building achievements, or the jobs—and revenue—she brought back to the state from Japan. Instead, they claimed I had bought her a truck with union funds. If they had dug a little deeper, they would have learned that the truck had been purchased for the new construction program. Had Marilyn driven it? Yes, but it was not *her* vehicle, any more than the vehicles driven by Michael Brittain or Amy Ejercito belonged to them.

Chapter 28

I wasn't the only labor guy who had a bad day on May 6. Stating that it didn't comply with the Kline-Miller Multiemployer Pension Reform Act of 2014, the Treasury Department denied the benefit suspension application of NY Teamsters Road Carriers Local 707, the Teamsters Central States, and Southeast & Southwest Areas Pension Fund. As mentioned earlier, the act, which was signed into law by President Obama in 2014, charged the Treasury Department with determining whether a pension was in danger of becoming insolvent, and if so, whether to reduce benefits until such time as the financial situation improved. Local 707 specifically stated in their application that the plan was within a few months of becoming insolvent.

In February of 2017, Local 707 became the first union pension to officially run out of money. As a result, four thousand former truckers had their pensions slashed, many of them drastically. Local 707 retirees would now receive their checks from the Pension Benefit Guaranty Corp, a government insurance company that bails out troubled pensions. I read about one guy who had gone from $48,000 a year to less than half that. He had paid into the pension for thirty years and was promised his pension would always be there, as it had been collectively bargained for. Some recalled getting letters as far back as fifteen years ago that the fund was in trouble. Yet the fiscal mismanagement continued, and now men well past retirement age had to scrounge to meet their monthly expenses. It made me sick.

And this was just the tip of the iceberg. The NY State Teamsters Pension Fund, with its 35,000 members, is in trouble, as are Teamster Locals 641 and 560 in New Jersey. The general counsel of the 407,000-member Central States Pension Fund has predicted a "tsunami" of municipal and state plans in danger of going down.

The PBGC is also at risk. It currently has $2 billion in assets, but it paid out $113 million in 2016 to support sixty-five bankrupt plans. Local 707 alone is costing them $1.7 million a month. One does not have to be a rocket scientist to know that such bailouts are not a long-term solution. In total, one million American workers are at risk of losing their pensions, all because labor leaders have been more concerned with keeping their jobs than making the tough decisions that would create a secure future.

This was exactly the sort of thing I sought to avoid for my staff. The pensions for Local 1260 staff members was managed by the National Electrical Annuity Plan (NEAP); I myself had been a member since 1992, and it was also in my interest to protect the monies. That's why I reduced the percentage of our contribution during the lean times. There was little I could do for the members in this regard, as the pensions were managed not by Local 1260 but by the individual employers. They, too, had to meet the standards of the 2014 law. There were a variety of plans out there—Servpro might have a 401k matching plan, while the Pacific Missile Range had a defined contribution plan, with the company matching 4 percent, and so on, and although I did not deal with them on a daily basis, I had to have working knowledge of each. I would negotiate certain parameters within the collective bargaining agreement with the understanding that the employer would notify me before making any changes.

When the economy tanked in 2008, Hawaiian Electric's plan had fallen below the "safety" line, but by 2012 it was again fully funded, which was how I was able to up the defined payout from $50,000 to $100,000, thereby giving workers the ability to pay down their bills, make an investment for their future, et cetera. After May 6, the IBEW accused me of acting solely for my benefit, when the truth was I had simply done what they could not. I saw the handwriting on the wall, then thought outside the box in order to protect my staff. We were, after all, also members of the IBEW.

• • •

Gradually, as I emerged from the fog of shock, loss, and despair, I began to piece it all together. Members of my staff—chief among them Russell Takemoto, Melanie Salvador, and Michael Brittain—had conspired with Harold Dias to get me out. In fact, Harold was the lynchpin here; he was the one who approached John O'Rourke about putting Local 1260 under trusteeship. I'm not sure how much convincing O'Rourke took, but I was betting that Harold said I was planning to run against him in the upcoming election for vice president of the Ninth District. It was, after all, the union way: get rid of your competition by any means necessary before they become a serious threat. These people, some of whom I had known for more than a decade, had sold me down the river without a second thought.

It wasn't hard to guess at the others' motives, either. Ever since Tommy's lawsuit, I'd been concerned about what my staff would do if I did not keep them on board. Turns out they did not wait for me to get rid of them; they got rid of me first. Michael Brittain, who had often told staffers he would be the next business manager, probably thought I would retire and appoint Brandon as my successor.

Russell Takemoto had been angry with me ever since I replaced him as chief of staff the year before; he had also noticed that I was running out of places to put him. Melanie was also afraid she might lose her job. I'd already mentioned that I was thinking of outsourcing the accounting work to an outside company.

Others, like Amy Ejercito, had likely known about the plot and said nothing to warn me. Since International had been sure to fire everyone loyal to me, I could safely assume that anyone working in the office after May 6 was not.

They even tried to drive a wedge between me and my own son. After I was kicked out, John O'Rourke had the gall to call Brandon. "If you want to come into the office, you can," he told him. It was a fishing expedition to see if he would turn on me.

"I don't think so," Brandon replied, managing to mask his own pain and outrage with a calm, collected tone. "We did nothing wrong."

Brandon took the IBEW's betrayal even harder than I had. Like me, he had grown up believing that labor was a force for good in the world; he had believed in it—and in me—so much that he had moved his family back to Hawaii to work with me. When May 6 happened, it was as if the union took not only his livelihood and his reputation, but his idealism as well. He had plenty of anger and sadness, though, and it was heartbreaking to watch, not only for me but for Marilyn and Neiani as well. I told myself that it was better for my son to have gotten this wake-up call in his early thirties, rather than his late fifties, and that he would soon rebound stronger than ever.

Even my son-in-law Eric was a casualty of the fallout. Though I had brought him on board just two months before being ousted, Eric was accused—and found guilty by the IBEW's "kangaroo court"—of all the things they'd accused me of. His punishment? He was expelled for life; he could never again be a member, an officer, or a staff member of the union. Apparently, the International never bothered to inform his local of this, for he remained on their rosters as a dues-paying member—and they are both located in DC! It was just another example of the dysfunction and lack of communication in the IBEW, and for me and my family, one of the few amusing aspects of this whole dirty business.

● ● ●

Even as the media worked to destroy my good name, the conspirators at the IBEW wasted no time in dismantling the model I'd built. Within days, the website had been purged of my presence, including the links to my YouTube videos. You would have thought I was promoting anarchy, rather than telling members to believe in themselves and the work they were doing. "Living 808"—which had been both a powerful morale booster for the members and a public relations tool—was also wiped out. As upsetting as these changes were, what went on behind the scenes was even worse.

The International chose Harold Dias as trustee, which meant that he would theoretically be doing my job every day. Had the betrayal not been so complete, this would have been a laughable notion. This was a man with a terrible track record with unions. After assuming the role of business manager of Local 1357 back in the late nineties, Harold had succeeded only in reducing the membership from 2,800 members to 700. He had literally never organized a single person in all his years with the IBEW. I thought back to 2014, when he had suggested using my model for unions across the country. It would have been a dream come true had DC not put the kibosh on it, and at the time I was impressed that Harold had pushed for it. We had been through a lot of ups and downs over the years, and though Harold and I disagreed about a great many things, I never thought he would do something like this to me.

As trustee and a loyalist to the International, Harold Dias basically had the authority to do what he wanted, and what he wanted most was to kill the fledgling construction division. I soon learned he had rented out the space set aside for that department and sold the furniture. He only rented out half of the main office space and sold that furniture as well. Did he do this to bring in revenue? If so, it was ironic that he got rid of a program that would have brought in a significant revenue stream. We already had new contracts coming in and had signed with Henkels and McCoy, an enormous construction company with locations throughout the country. As lineman jobs were extremely coveted, the apprenticeship program I had been putting together would have held an appeal for the younger generations, thereby increasing our membership roster for years to come.

Only slightly less shocking than the trusteeship was the feeble support I got from friends and colleagues, many of whom I had known for decades. Marilyn and I were deserted by all but three people who reached out to offer their support and friendship. I saw a whole new side to humanity, and it made me a bit sad. These people had known me and my family for years, yet they chose to believe what was in the news rather than the truth right in front of them. Some of these people had stayed in my home and benefitted from my leadership and kindness, both personally and professionally, but still, when everything hit the fan, they scurried away as fast as they could.

The same thing happened to Brandon, Neiani, and Jennifer, all of whom stayed in Hawaii after Marilyn and I left. Since returning, Neiani had participated in the Great Aloha Run, an 8.15-mile walk/run for charity. It had been going on for the past thirty or forty years and drew people from all over the world. Like any marathon, aid stations were placed along the route where participants could get water. As she approached one of these stations, she spotted John Gomes, a former treasurer on the executive board and a close friend of Jennifer. When he saw Neiani coming toward him, he literally ran in the other direction.

This is a person who used to stop by the office at five a.m. just to say hello. When he took trips to the mainland, we would pick him up from the airport. He was particularly close to my sister-in-law Jennifer; he called her all the time, even when they had no business to discuss. If I'd thought anyone would remain loyal to me and my family after May 6, it was John Gomes. Instead, he completely cut all of us off. He no longer reached out to Jennifer, and he didn't take her calls either; any messages she left him went unanswered. His behavior angered me, probably even more so because he placed self-preservation over friendship. He could think whatever he wanted about me, but there was no way he really believed that my sister-in-law had done anything underhanded.

Of all the things my family lost on May 6, one of the most painful was Hawaii itself. The theft of Local 1260, with all that entailed, coupled with the lack of support from my fellow Hawaiians, was difficult to reconcile with the place of warmth and camaraderie in which I had grown up. After a month or so of enduring the attacks of the local media and the cold shoulder from our so-called friends and allies, Marilyn and I had had enough. We thought things might improve when, after investigating the International's claims against me and my family, the state of Hawaii found absolutely no evidence of wrongdoing. The media, however, did not bother to exonerate us; it was simply not worth their time.

So, with heavy hearts, we packed up our things and headed for our house in Nevada.

In and of itself, leaving Hawaii was not a hardship; in fact, since becoming an International rep in 2003, I had probably spent more time on the mainland. Even after I returned from DC and became business manager, I was always travelling; all told, I spent only about half the year at home.

Marilyn and I hadn't planned on retiring on Hawaii, either. It was too expensive, for one, with the median price of a home over $700,000. Everyday goods were also exorbitant—a gallon of milk could cost as much as seven dollars!—and many islanders eventually settled in Nevada and other states so they could live more comfortably. The mainland also offered convenience. Travel would be much easier from Nevada, as would pursuing new career opportunities. For some time Brandon and I had talked about one day starting our own business, and now that we were both free of the union, the conversation took a much more serious tone. Given the hatchet job the IBEW and the media did on us, Hawaii was definitely not the best place for us to get our venture off the ground.

I would always cherish the memories of my childhood, as well as the pristine beaches and incredible sunsets, but we made the decision as a family that it was time to move on. The betrayal and abandonment by those we considered close friends and colleagues left stains on our hearts. At one of the many family meetings we would have after May 6, Marilyn, Brandon, Neiani, and I decided that once our names were cleared, we would vacation in Hawaii, but we would never live there again.

Chapter 29

Throughout this whole mess, one thing brought me solace: I left Local 1260 a vastly different place than I had found it. Local 1260, back when I started in 1979, had 1,900 members. In 2016, when I was robbed of my office, we were 3,000 strong; this included a thousand workers I had personally organized. I also negotiated more than 350 contracts over the course of my career, thereby improving the lives of our members by increasing benefits, market share, and union density. As business manager and financial secretary, I had transformed the local from a place of fiscal and public relations stagnancy into a successful model of what labor could be, and I had done it in less than five years. It was not about getting accolades from the International or the community—though I had gotten both—but knowing in my heart that I had done everything within my power to make the members' experience a worthwhile one.

This model was also sustainable, and, if run correctly, could have changed the face of labor in this country, one local at a time. The fact that the International had put the kibosh on it could not dampen my pride. I firmly believe that the working men and women are the backbone of America; without them, we would have the same polarities between rich and poor that our forefathers sought to escape.

Passion and perseverance is in their blood, and no matter what obstacles they face, they always seem to prevail. Unions could have been part of their success, not by creating division between workers and their employers, but by understanding that the success of one was inextricably linked to the other. This meant seeing companies not as evil entities making profits off the backs of workers, but organizations simply trying to survive—and thrive—in a competitive world. I am not stating a political platitude, but a reality. As my father realized decades ago, advocating for workers meant more than simply demanding higher and more fringe benefits regardless of the surrounding circumstances. Negotiators must always have their ears to the ground and their eyes on the future, keeping in mind potential changes to an industry and other factors that could affect the employer as well as the employee. If a company went out of business because it could not afford to pay its overhead (i.e. exorbitant wages), everybody lost.

In refusing to acknowledge these truths, labor has made itself largely irrelevant in this country. One only has to see the decline in union density to see that. For years I continued to hope that things would change; I even tried to be that change. Since becoming business manager I had taken responsibility for everything that occurred on my watch. Every blunder by a staff member, every missed opportunity to improve in some way (because everything can be improved), I believed ultimately landed at my feet. Ironically, it would be May 6, one of the worst days of my life, to release me from this burden. Local 1260 would not continue to run on my model; it would be swallowed up by the slow yet deliberate steamroller known as the IBEW. The realization that I could not stop it was surprisingly liberating. I was still devastated by what had happened, of course, but I found myself taking a step back and truly looking at all the ways in which Local 1260 had positively affected the community. When I walked out of that office on May 6, that day we had over three thousand members. If that number (or anything else) declined after that, it would have nothing to do with me. This was the beginning of the turning point, the moment at which I decided that no matter what the IBEW threw at me, I would remain standing.

Though I could have fought the International's decision to remove me as business manager, I never even went to a hearing. I was officially entitled to one, but all the union rules and regulations around it would have whittled my rights down to nothing. I would only be able to use a union member as an attorney, and the very guys who had stolen Local 1260 from me would serve as my judge and jury. If I wanted to appeal their decision, I would have to go before the International Executive Council, of which all eight members were appointed by the president of the IBEW, who had ordered the takeover in the first place. Imagine an organization supposedly dedicated to workers' rights that does not have an impartial system to adjudicate disputes within its ranks! It reminded me of those International reps who had tried to organize and create a "union within a union," only to be crushed by the International. The hypocrisy was mind-boggling.

I did engage three different private attorneys, all of whom told me not to say anything because it would only be dignifying the process.

The best option, they told me, was for this debacle to go through a third party.

"Do you want to go back there?" one of them asked me. "Because I can get you back. This is all a scam."

I paused for all of two seconds, then said, "I don't want to go back. I just want my pension and my medical benefits."

That would turn out to be another battle. For the next several months, during their "investigation," my benefits hung in the balance. Eventually, the IBEW did release my pension, but for reasons still unknown to me I have not recovered my medical benefits. Ironically, the medical benefits for Local 1260's staff were one of the things I had changed while business manager so I could protect retirees while saving the active members money.

To be honest, I wanted one more thing. Underneath the hurt and confusion lurked a rough and tumble union guy, just itching for a fight. For those first few weeks I often thought about what I would like to do to those who had betrayed me. I had dirt on almost all of them—some of it dating back years or even decades—that could ruin careers and alliances. Sometimes, my thoughts ran darker still. I could beat them, I thought more than once, and just wait for the cops to come. Then sanity would return, and I'd remember that a fleeting moment of revenge—no matter how sweet—was not worth a lifetime of regret. I started thinking less about what I wanted to do and more about what God would want. One thing was for sure, He would not want me to engage in the same Neanderthal tactics as those who had wronged me. He would want me to take the high road and have faith that He would intervene on my behalf. This was not about "turning the other cheek," but about climbing out of the pit and letting them know they had not defeated me. That would be the best revenge.

• • •

Mike Mowrey used to say that I was an anomaly because of all I accomplished in my career. While I appreciate the compliment, great achievement shouldn't be out of the ordinary. Yes, I accomplished a great deal, and I feel blessed that God put me in a position to help so many people and effect change. It has always been my belief that He created each of us with a purpose; it is our right and our responsibility to find that purpose and live it with passion. When any organization, whether it be a labor union, company, or government, tries to stamp out that flame, it is time for that organization to either change or dissolve. That is the crossroads at which labor stands now, and has for the past few decades. Somewhere along the lines labor leaders got stuck in a rut; they do the same thing, the same way, and get the same result, to the detriment not only of the members but of the country as a whole. Union density statistics bear this out. At the time of this writing, private sector unions have fallen to the 6.4% range. That means 93.6% of all private sector workers in this country are *nonunion*. That's a slide from 7.9 % one year ago. Even Hawaii, one of the most prounion states in the nation, has dropped below 20 percent, and the decline continues. No new ideas circulate to increase membership. Labor truly is not the preferred choice for workers anymore. Workers know that unions are antiquated and have lost their way. Leadership will never change.

Yet somehow labor leaders have been able to hang on to their political and economic power, guarding their turf and viciously crushing anyone who dares to find a better way of serving the members. For-profit companies do not have this luxury; in order to remain competitive, they must continually reevaluate what they are doing right and areas in which they can improve with regard to their respective industries, particularly those directly affected by technological advances. They must embrace changes and open themselves up to new ways of doing things, sometimes to the point of completely reinventing and rebranding themselves. If they do not, they will be held accountable by the consumer.

The same is true for individuals; and this was the position I found myself in after May 6. After a lifetime in the union, I had to decide who I was without it. Fortunately for me, I have never been afraid of introspection, and when I moved past the initial shock—if not the devastation and anger—of what had happened, I saw the truth of the situation much easier. Local 1260, and the new model I had created for it, had been stolen out of pure jealousy and the need to control. It had nothing to do with my worth or the work I believe I am here to do: assist workers and their employers communicate with respect for the highest good of both parties. I did not need a union to do this. And with that in mind, I rolled up my sleeves and went to work building a business in the private sector. And I would do it with my family by my side.

I have always believed that our lowest moments, when things we hold dear are stripped away, can also provide our greatest opportunities for previously unimagined growth, evolution, and success. A few months after the IBEW unjustly fired them, Brandon and Neiani started Mitch's Wai Ehu Chili Pepper Water, a company that manufactures and distributes chili pepper water for sale in Hawaii and online. And in late 2016, my son and I realized our dream of going into business together. Our company, the Global Institute for Interest-Based Solutions, is founded on our shared passion for facilitating communication and cohesiveness between employers and employees so they can strive together toward prosperity without the interference of a union or other third party. We audit the company, searching for any issues among the different levels of management, and between management and employees. If we find none, we report that to the company, and our work is done. However, if we find issues, we explain them to management and present a plan of how we can help. The goal is to train management, all the way from shift supervisor to CEO, and educate workers so they can come together as equal partners for the benefit of all.

This is much more than "union avoidance." Since beginning this work I found that many consultants were also former union guys who for whatever reason had soured on labor and now wanted to strike out at it. They would go into a company and essentially badmouth unions, listing all the reasons why unions are "bad," much the same as labor has always done with employers. In either case, this is not productive unless another way to move forward is also provided. The Global

Institute is not about fighting problems, but achieving the goals set out by the company for the benefit of workers and management. If after doing our assessment we find a legitimate reason for the union to be there, we will not dispute it. If, however, a company comes to us and says, "The union is adversarial and the employees don't like it, but we have a union security clause—can you help us?" then we can step in to educate them about their options.

That said, neither I nor management would ever attempt to lock the union out or prevent workers from organizing. This is illegal, and in my opinion, immoral, for it is up to employees to make this determination on their own. If, however, they come to the conclusion that they no longer need or want to be part of a union, they can go to NLRB themselves and decertify. Ultimately, it is about their empowerment and self-determination.

Chapter 30

In the months following, I continued to pay close attention to the presidential campaign. There was no doubt that Donald Trump had incited a revolution within the Republican Party, but even as I watched him make speech after grandiose speech, I didn't think too much of it. Some of what he said made sense, but it seemed as though he had alienated far too many people with his rhetoric about everything from healthcare to "building the wall." He did have quite a bit of support among certain demographics, particularly in Middle America, but this was downplayed in the mainstream media. The polls also seemed to indicate that Hillary had several distinct paths to the White House, while Trump's chances of getting the necessary electoral votes were slim to none.

His victory on November 8, 2016, shocked me as much as it did any other American, but perhaps for different reasons. After so many years in the union, I was used to people maintaining the status quo, settling for a safe, controlled descent rather than change that had the potential to create growth, and I guess I expected the same of the American people in choosing their next leader. Instead, the electorate sent a resounding message to Washington. They were tired of the stalemates and the fighting along party lines. Our political system is broken and, faced with two obviously flawed candidates, they were going to choose the outsider. This message was even more profound in the labor community; while labor leaders were divided during the primary season between Hillary Clinton and Bernie Sanders, they solidly threw their support behind Clinton once she got the nomination. They assumed their members would follow suit, but when workers went to the polls, between 30 and 40 percent of them broke with their own leadership to vote for Trump. They, too, had decided they did not want a typical politician, but an outsider who would stir things up, even if that outsider made it a goal to break the back of the unions. Though I had not voted for him and had great trepidations about what he would do in office, the very fact that he had won seemed to indicate that others agreed with my view that something needed to change, both in labor and in Washington, DC, in general. The question remains, are those in power willing to put themselves out on a limb to effect that change for the rest of us? If they would just take that leap, there is literally nothing this country could not achieve.

Around the same time, another presumed "fait acompli" did not come to pass. After I was removed from office, the NextEra buyout of Hawaiian Electric, which I had vigorously supported after locking in protections for Locals 1260 and 1186, was voted down by the Public Utilities Commission. The decision left Hawaiian Electric once again holding the proverbial bag—meaning they had to figure out how to remain solvent and make the much-needed overhaul to the infrastructure of Hawaii's electrical grid. Raising rates is not an option, as they already have the highest in the country. This is one more thing I have had to let go of since leaving Local 1260. Though I am no longer a Hawaii resident, I still care deeply about the company and its workers, and I pray it all works out for them in the end. The contract I negotiated will remain in place until 2018, so at least I know I did all I could for them.

• • •

In this book I have discussed at length the decline and eventual demise of labor in America; however, it does not have to be this way. A progressive model moving forward would claim a niche for labor and get an engaged workforce that wants to be in the union, as associates not hostages. To do so will require a "purge" of sorts. Unions must get rid of the current leadership and elect new, younger, forward-thinking people who have a better understanding of the world's demographics and what workers want in today's society. In other words, they must be willing to run the union more like those corporations they love to vilify. If they did so, they would not only survive, but grow and thrive.

As radical as it sounds, they would also have to get rid of the jurisdictions that divide the unions; this would eliminate much of the politics and in-fighting that occurs when, as I saw, the construction local is vying with the electrical local for work. Even more radical is my proposal to "open shop" the entire labor movement. Do away with union security clauses altogether, and they can begin to move forward with a model that provides benefits that draw employees who truly want to be in the union, rather than those who are forced to do so. The resulting agreements with employees would honor the interests of *all* parties, rather than those of union leaders.

This new model should feature benefit structures that are not only attractive but imperative in today's society. These include scholarships so workers can educate themselves and their families; on-the-job education, retraining and apprenticeships; childcare services; and community service to foster camaraderie among members and give back to the public. It would also feature various types of medical and insurance benefits, including life insurance, car insurance, a way to buy supplemental health insurance from an outside company, and a fund for unemployment beyond the existing unemployment insurance already provided for. It should also provide a type of defined contribution pension plan and a savings plan that empowers members by encouraging their direct involvement so they know they are contributing to the goals.

This, of course, is in addition to the collective bargaining already handled by unions and includes bargaining to protect minority factions within the union. The union could also serve as legal counsel and go before the NLRB to advocate for workers who need workman's comp or temporary disability. Members could choose and pay for the services a la carte, according to their individual needs. For example, if someone wants to know that in the event of a layoff the union will help them with unemployment, he/she could pay five dollars a month for that.

Of course, the mere thought of competing on the open market terrifies labor leaders; they know that if they were to do this, many members would leave the union. Is this a risk? Of course it is. However, I have learned that one must be willing to let go of what one has in order to reach for more. Yes, members may leave at first, and who could blame them? Perhaps they have been paying dues for years and have seen no returns on their investment. Now they want to leave, and no amount of convincing will change their minds. Understand that this is okay; in fact, it is a healthy part of the process and the beginning of a new model of change and growth.

If union leaders would only open their hearts and minds to these changes, they would once again stand as powerful advocates for the workers who serve as the backbone of this country. Moreover, these workers would be empowered with knowledge and the ability to apply that knowledge so they can attain their slice of the American dream, however they envision it.

As I write this, I can hardly believe that nearly a year has passed since the IBEW placed Local 1260 under trusteeship. My journey has been a miraculous one, filled with twists and turns, and though it has been challenging and sometimes even painful, I know it has all been part of God's plan. Today my heart is full by the amazing ways in which my life has changed. My family is not only intact, but even stronger and closer than we were before this happened. And perhaps because we were so cruelly treated by those in power, we have all embarked on an entrepreneurial path—not just Brandon and me, but Marilyn and our daughter Megan as well. Their company,

Simply Staging Designs, stages homes in preparation for sale. Jenn, my sister-in-law, is also thriving in a new, fulfilling career in elderly care. I will be honest, I am still deeply wounded by the way the IBEW treated me after thirty-five years of service; however, I now know that the acute phase of that pain is over, and thanks to family and God, it will all be—not just okay—but wonderful.

How did I get to this place in less than a year? By following the same few but profound principles I have always lived by, regardless of my circumstances. In order to keep moving forward in life, it is imperative that you take risks. I am not advocating erratic or impulsive behavior, but action based on a combination of a logical calculation and a gut feeling about what is right. I did this throughout my career with the IBEW, both in Hawaii and in DC, not because I was looking for accolades, but because I felt it was in the best interest of the members. Building the media center without any customers was a risk, but as people started to use it, to participate in the vision, that was all the validation I needed. The same was true of the construction training center, which I built even though I didn't have the construction jurisdiction or the people for the apprenticeship program. When people came and saw the pathway and the opportunities the program would create, I did not need them to compliment me. Their interest and excitement was enough to fill me with joy.

The key is that when you are guided not by praise from others but by your internal compass, God will take you in the right direction. Now, this does not mean that the "right direction" will always show up the way you expected, but if you have faith and stay the course, you will find that what happens is better than anything you could have imagined or dreamed of. While this "rogue attitude" arguably contributed to my demise at the union, I maintain that the successes on behalf of others were well worth it. Did I have moments of doubt, when I thought it would have been easier to keep my head down until I could collect my pension? If course I did, but then I would have been forfeiting a life of passion and purpose and instead choosing one of inertia and apathy. I saw enough of that in DC to know I never wanted to end up that way.

As is true in life, so is true in business. In my model of success, the employer and employee do not need validation from each other. Why? Because the results of their communication speaks for itself. When you build a business with an open heart and mind, you do not need a pat on the back. Your relationship with your employees, and your bottom line, will be all the validation you need. The same is true of the Global Institute for Interest-Based Solutions. Brandon and I get no greater satisfaction than when we teach others that they have the ability to succeed without us holding their hand. They have the ability to stand with confidence, without justification from others. You must trust that the end product is enough to move you forward. You must be okay with yourself.

Another thing that facilitated my healing after May 6 was getting involved in the community and helping others. I joined a group at my church called "This Man Is You." Each Saturday we meet before nine a.m. mass for lectures and roundtable discussions about how we can help local youth or serve in some other way.

Helping people also keeps us connected, which is especially important after being wounded by another's actions. One Sunday morning, I stopped at a grocery store near my home to buy ingredients for breakfast. Ahead of me in line was a girl about ten or twelve years old, and I immediately took note of her huge glasses, messy hair, and pajamas. Someone had sent her in, I thought, as she pulled out a baggy containing four dollar bills and some change, someone who lived in a car. My granddaughter's face flashed through my head, and I could only pray someone would help her. Then I took out a twenty, paid for her food, and gave her the change. For the grateful smile she gave me before running out of the store, I would have given her ten times that.

If I've learned anything from my experiences, it is that it is incumbent upon us to take in *all* that life gives us—not just that which is to our liking . We must experience the journey that God has set for us. If we embrace the good with the bad, the beauty and ugliness, the truthfulness and the deceit, we will learn from each experience we have and each action we take. The important thing is never to react on impulse, but to take a step back and determine the path that keeps us whole and strong. Never let life's obstacles keep you down; instead, let those obstacles be your strength to grow, to improve, to increase your sharing, and to love more with all your heart. I have always believed that God is watching over all of us and that He has a divine plan for each of us. He keeps us safe.

Like everyone else, I have had my moments of pain and confusion about my journey; I have felt "forsaken," not by God, but by others I have sought to help. Then I remind myself that we all are here to live with passion and purpose, not just when things are going our way, but each and every day. And in those moments of doubt, I turn to the words of a woman who dedicated her entire life to uplifting the world—Mother Theresa:

People are often unreasonable, illogical, and self-centered;
Forgive them anyway.

If you are kind, people may accuse you of selfish, ulterior motives;
Be kind anyway.

If you are successful, you will win some false friends and some
true enemies;
Succeed anyway.

If you are honest and frank, people may cheat you;
Be honest and frank anyway.

What you spend years building, someone could destroy overnight;
Build anyway.

If you find serenity and happiness, they may be jealous;
Be happy anyway.

The good you do today, people will often forget tomorrow;
Do good anyway.

Give the world the best you have, and it may never be enough;
Give the world the best you've got anyway.

You see, in the final analysis, it is between you and your God;
It was never between you and them anyway.